MARCO  POLO

C000205129

INDIA SOUTH

GOA & KERALA

SYMBOLS

INSIDER TIP   Insider Tip
★   Highlight
●●●●   Best of ...
☼   Scenic view
☺   Responsible travel: fair
              trade principles and the
              environment respected
(*)   Telephone numbers
              that are not toll-free

**PRICE CATEGORIES
HOTELS**

Expensive	over 5,600 Rs
Moderate	2,800 – 5,600 Rs
Budget	under 2,800 Rs

The prices are for two people
sharing per night, including
breakfast

**PRICE CATEGORIES
RESTAURANTS**

Expensive	over 1,000 Rs
Moderate	500 – 1,000 Rs
Budget	under 500 Rs

The prices are for a main
meal without drinks

On the cover: The splendour of the maharajas p. 91 | In the Tiger Reserve p. 117

CONTENTS

Karnataka → p. 74

Tamil Nadu → p. 94

Trips & Tours → p. 114

Road atlas → p. 138

DID YOU KNOW?
Timeline → p. 12
Local specialities → p. 26
Kathakali → p. 53
Books & Films → p. 84
Currency converter → p. 131
Budgeting → p. 132
Weather in Goa → p. 134

MAPS IN THE GUIDEBOOK
(140 A1) Page numbers and
coordinates refer to the road
atlas
(0) Site/address located off
the map.
Coordinates are also given for
places that are not marked
on the road atlas
Maps of Bengaluru, Chennai,
Panaji and Thiruvananthapuram
are found inside the back cover
Map of Kochi → p. 48

**INSIDE BACK COVER:
PULL-OUT MAP →**

PULL-OUT MAP 🗺
(🗺 A–B 2–3) Refers to the
removable pull-out map

The best MARCO POLO Insider Tips

Our top 15 Insider Tips

INSIDER TIP Saturday night in Goa
While others sleep, in Goa you can go shopping instead. Enjoy a very special atmosphere, partying, bartering and marvelling at the Arpora Saturday Night Bazaar → p. 36

INSIDER TIP City of the future
Spiritual freedom through yoga and meditation at the Sri Aurobindo ashram in Auroville. Around 2000 people from 40 countries live in this 'universal city' → p. 104, 123

INSIDER TIP Romance under the stars
The Full Moon Restaurant on Bogmalo Bay sets up tables right at the water's edge → p. 41

INSIDER TIP From villains to conservationists
Go walk-about with former ivory smugglers and poachers in Thekkady: no one is more familiar with the tracks of the elephants, or can better spot the signs of a tiger → p. 117

INSIDER TIP Thousands of coconuts for Ganesh
Every morning, offerings are taken to the elephant-headed god at the Pazhavangadi Ganapathy Temple → p. 66

INSIDER TIP Cruising into the sunset
Happy hour: the right place and the right time for an evening excursion on the Mandovi River, live music, Goan dancing and dinner included → p. 42

INSIDER TIP The perfect fit in one hour
Skirts, blouses, trousers or shirts: at the Pudumandapam Market in Madurai there are 250 tailors who'll make up your garments in no time at all → p. 106

INSIDER TIP Hot & spicy
Nutmeg, cardamom, vanilla, cinnamon and sandalwood – exotic fragrances at the spice market in Kochi → p. 51

INSIDER TIP Steaming through the hills

It looks like a toy – and doesn't go much faster. Thank goodness, because now you can lean back and enjoy the nostalgia trip to Ooty aboard the Nilgiri Mountain Railway. Look out for the monkeys along the route, and share your lunch with fellow passengers (photo left) → p. 114

INSIDER TIP Avoiding the crowds

In the Nilgiri Mountains, you've (still) got the mountain caves and dense jungle of the pristine Wayanad National Park almost all to yourself (photo below) → p. 64

INSIDER TIP Relaxing among the bananas

In Hampi, travellers congregate at the Mango Tree to eat delicious and cheap *thalis.* Then they sit and relax while overlooking the river – sometimes for the whole afternoon → p. 82

INSIDER TIP Feeding time for an elephant

Twice a day at the Aarathy restaurant in Madurai, guests can feed the temple elephant with South Indian specialities → p. 106

INSIDER TIP Holiday on the farm

Certainly not something you would immediately associate with a trip to this part of the world: life on the farm Indian style. Learn about organic farming, drive an ox-cart and also immerse yourself in the holistic spa at the village near Bengaluru → p. 79

INSIDER TIP Frolicking around

In the evening, dolphins come out to play in the sea off the secluded Agonda beach → p. 38

INSIDER TIP Sleeping under elephant grass

With the inclusion of natural materials, the cottages of the Spice Village in Thekkady make for a healthy environment, perfect for a good night's sleep → p. 58

BEST OF ...

FOR FREE

● *An early start to the day with yoga*
From 6–8am, at 26 different public spaces in Chennai, e.g. Panagal Park and Marina Beach, you can take part in *free yoga classes*. The idea came from the former mayor, who had the good health of the citizenry at heart → p. 123

● *Massage included*
In the spice gardens of Goa, tours also include free, relaxing *massages*. Of course, there is the ulterior motive that you'll later purchase the requisite oils, but you don't have to → p. 43

● *Silent Parties*
Dancing at night, barefoot on the sand, with headphones on – that's both romantic and considerate. And it's easy on the wallet: the *open air discos in Palolem* in Goa offer free entry (photo) → p. 39

● *First the rice harvest, then the entertainment*
Once the rice has been gathered in, the farmers around Hampi organise *ox-cart races* and *bullfights*. The animals don't suffer, the Torero's prize being the money and sweets that he manages to pluck from the head of the bull. And you can also take part and enjoy South Indian traditions up close → p. 83

● *End the day with fresh shrimps*
Buy some freshly caught shrimps straight from the Chinese fishing nets in Kochi and have them prepared at the stall. They'll cost you a pound at most and you'll sit on the sand with the bag in your hand and watch as the giant nets are silhouetted against the sunset – just stunning → p. 50

● *More than 300 concerts for free*
At the *Chennai Music and Dance Festival*, classical music and traditional dances are performed at more than 100 venues, with over 2000 participants contributing to at least 300 concerts. And it doesn't cost a thing, though small donations are, of course, always welcome → p. 127

●●●● Dots in guidebook refer to 'Best of ...' tips

ONLY IN SOUTH INDIA
Unique experiences

● *When Indian men go dancing*
Kathakali, the best-known dance drama in South India, is noted for the colourful make-up and elaborate costumes of the male-only performers. You are welcome to watch the painstaking make-up process, and of course the dances themselves, which recreate scenes from ancient Hindu epics → p. 53

● *Temporary tattoo*
In the model village of *Dakshinachitra* near Chennai, you can see demonstrations of typical Indian handicrafts. While you're there, you can also have elaborate henna mehndi patterns painted on your hands → p. 102

● *Spiritual shopping*
Pondicherry is a real shopper's paradise when it comes to basic spiritual requirements. This is mainly due to the *Sri Aurobindo shops,* which sell clothes, bags, jewellery, incense sticks, oils and high quality handmade paper, all made in the nearby ashram at Auroville → p. 104

● *India's treasures lie in the south*
The vast majority of the subcontinent's most impressive monuments and cultural treasures are located in South India. Look out for the stunning *temple complex of Hampi* (photo) and the magical *sea temple in Mamallapuram* → p. 80, 103

● *Riding pillion through Goa*
When in Goa you can hire a motorbike rider who will take you everywhere on the back of his bike or Vespa. It's inexpensive, fun and an unusual way to get around. You can find *two-wheeler taxi stands* everywhere → p. 41

● *Farewell on the beach*
These *ceremonies* may make you feel uneasy, but will show you a real piece of India. You have to get up early though to watch the priests at work on *Varkala beach* in Kerala. Families arrive with the ashes of their recently departed, so they can be blessed and then scattered in the sea → p. 68

ONLY IN

BEST OF ...

● *Walking in the rain*
The hill tribes of northeast Kerala celebrate the monsoon rains with particular abandon. And you can join in too, with walks in the rain, mud football or crab races → p. 64

● *Shopping South Indian style*
Forget about a flying visit. You can get lost in the covered bazaar near the *Sri Meenakshi Sundareshwarar Temple* in Madurai. Time flies as you wander among all the fragrances, colours and gorgeous materials → p. 106

● *Doubly effective*
Because the warm damp opens up pores in the skin, Ayurveda practitioners believe the monsoon to be the best time of year for a cure. There is the additional consideration that patients can concentrate fully on their treatments, rather than swim or sunbathe (photo) → p. 44

● *More than Bollywood*
Indian movies are not just Bollywood. And every small town has its own cinema, where the audience enthusiastically participates, laughing, crying and clapping. Go along and experience it all at first hand – in Chennai, Ooty and many other places → p. 101, 112

● *Market for all the senses*
Around the halls of the *Devaraja Fruit & Vegetable Market* in Mysore you'll experience the real India. Sample the juicy (peeled) tropical fruits, take photographs of the colourful spice cones, close your eyes and absorb the intense floral scents → p. 92

● *The power of water*
The *Jog Falls* in Karnataka are at their most impressive during the monsoon season. Then the six separate cascades merge into one, as enormous quantities of water drop thunderously to depths of 250m (800ft) → p. 87

RAIN

RELAX AND CHILL OUT
Take it easy and spoil yourself

● *Relax with a good conscience*

The legendary Om Beach is the location of the *Swaswara Yoga and Ayurveda Resort*. In this charming hotel they don't just focus on your wellbeing, but thanks to strict environmental guidelines also take care of the surroundings – a totally holistic experience → **p. 90**

● *Dine in peaceful harmony*

At the thatched *Blue Ginger Restaurant* in Bangalore those travelling alone have a goldfish delivered to the table in a bowl. Such a dining partner aids relaxation: you don't have to make conversation and you can still have pleasant company → **p. 77**

● *Paradise from a boat*

The *Pichavaram Forest* near Chidambaram is the world's second-largest mangrove forest and a unique place for ecotourism. The boat takes you right away from civilisation and through a luxuriant wilderness → **p. 104**

● *Vantage point*

The best place to chill for the evening is in an *open air café on the Varkala cliffs* in Kerala. Sit with your feet up in the first row, as you watch the sun dipping into the sea. And enjoy the spectacular panoramic view out to sea and over the sand, which soon becomes a stage for entranced dancers → **p. 69**

● *In good hands*

A visit to the *Millennium Beauty Parlour* in Margao is an all-round, feel-good experience. You can spend an entire day here, with natural hair packs and wonderful massages and peelings → **p. 39**

● *Chilling out on a houseboat*

In the gloriously enchanting *Backwaters of Kerala*, the best and most relaxing way to enjoy the tropical environment with its rich flora and fauna is from the deck of a houseboat. During the journey, they will spoil you with delicious regional specialities, freshly prepared on board (photo) → **p. 72**

INTRODUCTION

DISCOVER SOUTH INDIA!

South India gets under your skin. It's a place where the air is soft and velvety, full of promise. Those who really engage with it will also learn much about themselves. A journey through this magical, sensory land is like visiting your inner self. Witness a temple ceremony and you are likely to lose all sense of time and space. Watching the fishermen putting out to the Arabian Sea in their ancient catamarans, you will feel as if you are in a time warp. Ayurvedic oil massages can help to induce a state of weightlessness, and everywhere you go, bustle and stress are replaced by a much calmer rhythm. And then there are the smiles, which are so infectious that in the end you just can't resist.

Whether landing in Chennai (Madras), in Panaji, in Bengaluru (Bangalore) or in Thiruvananthapuram (Trivandrum), new arrivals will be almost bowled over by a surge of exotic images. Heavy is the smell of coconut in the palm groves of Kerala, mixed with the opium-sweet fragrance of the white almond blossom. Traffic congestion in the cities, accompanied by a continuous blaring of horns, takes some getting

Photo: Fishing along the Backwaters of Kerala

used to. Apparent contradictions are a matter of course for locals. Even in the remotest areas, you will find a phone shop with ISDN on every corner and at least one internet café. And women wearing traditional saris but talking into a mobile phone is a common sight on the streets. Rolling into Mysore aboard the *Golden Chariot* luxury train, you will have a close encounter with the poorest of the poor sleeping on the station platform. But only tourists bother to take any notice of them. In contrast, the number

The Europeans grabbed territory for themselves

of willing hands who seem to know exactly what guests want, is extravagant by European standards. South India is at first tiring, because it assaults the senses in such an unfamiliar way. Relaxation will only begin when you start to let go and open your mind to the region's intoxicating mix – the memory will stay with you forever.

Over the course of the centuries, conquerors from Europe were keen to grab a slice of India for themselves: the Dutch, the Portuguese the English and the French ... No wonder, this was fertile ground that yielded enough fruit and spices, as well as precious minerals, to operate a roaring trade. And all the main world religions gained a foothold here: Hinduism, Buddhism, Christianity, Islam, Zoroastrianism and to a lesser extent Judaism. Thanks to bounteous harvests and fish-rich waters, there is much less poverty in South India than in the more barren north. The level of education is higher, and in Kerala illiteracy hardly exists. Especially exciting is the mix of

268–233 BC
King Ashoka rules over the entire Indian empire

AD 550–1190
Start of the Indian Middle Ages, with the rise of South India

1498
Navigator and explorer Vasco da Gama lands at Calicut in present-day Kerala, thereby ushering in the colonial period

1746
The French conquer Madras

From 1756
From its bases in Calcutta, Madras and Bombay, the British East India Company subjugates large parts of India

Portuguese legacy: snow-white Baroque churches dominate Goa's cities

cultures. While young whizz-kids are busy developing their software in Bangalore, around 250km (155mi) away in the Nilgiri Mountains the Toda tribe still clings to its ancient traditions that have been handed down for thousands of years. Like a magnet for people all over the world, sadhus, gurus and yogis attract those in search of life's meaning. In many ashrams, pilgrims follow the teachings and vision of their master. Auroville near Pondicherry was founded in 1968 by Mother Mira Alfassa, the wife of the philosopher Sri Aurobindo. Today, her model spiritual commune accommodates around 2200 people from more than 47 countries.

At one time, visitors to South India were either student travellers or here for a beach holiday. Nowadays, people tend to have broader interests and hardly anyone staying

1858
Control of India passes from the East India Company to the British Crown, whose representative is the Viceroy

1877
The British Queen Victoria becomes Empress of India

1885
Founding of the National Congress

1920
Mahatma Gandhi calls for the non-violent overthrow of British rule

1947
India gains independence. Jawaharlal Nehru is the first prime minister

at the beaches of Goa or Kerala will come away without at least having taken a stroll through the historic Old Goa or seeing the magnificent Padmanabha Swamy Temple in Kerala's capital, Trivandrum. Anyone interested in the living history and architecture of holy sites will be impressed by the sea temples of Mamallapuram, by the stunning temple complex of Hampi, the fairytale palace of the Maharajas in Mysore and the magnificent Meenakshi temple in Madurai.

Many hotels, even small ones, are more than just somewhere to spend the night. Often there will be an Indian version of a spa zone with at least one massage table or a few magic tinctures to revive tired feet and weary spirits. More effective over the long term are Ayurveda treatments involving special diets, which can work wonders – provided you stick rigidly to the regime. Increasing numbers of outdoor enthusiasts and eco-tourists head for the larger national parks to 'shoot' elephants and leopards on their photo safaris: in game reserves like Periyar in Kerala; Molem

All the great world religions gained a foothold

and Bhagvan Mahavir, which straddles the border between Goa, Karnataka, Kerala and Tamil Nadu in the Western Ghats; in Bandipur, Nagarhole and Kabini in Karnataka. Trekking tours take in the enchanted world of the jungle and rainforest. Kerala's Backwaters, the dense network of almost 2000km (1250mi) of waterways, lakes and lagoons, create another unique attraction. Over a thousand houseboats in Alappuzha wait on tourists to take them along what were once important commercial transport arteries.

And all visitors succumb to the temptation that is shopping. Almost every holidaymaker flies home with double the amount of luggage. Tea straight from the factory, spices from colourful markets, decorative statues of gods made out of bronze or sandalwood, silk blouses, cotton fabrics with exotic designs, pashmina shawls, real gold and silver jewellery, and sparkling false gold. The cotton and silk fabrics from Chennai (Madras) and nearby Kanchipuram are among the most beautiful and finest materials to be found in all India. Chennai is also the centre of the leather industry. Because most products are exported to the west, you can also find all the latest fashion in the shops, at prices well below what you'd pay in London. As a shopper's paradise, India simply can't be beaten.

1950 Indian Constitution adopted

1956 The former princely states of Cochin, Malabar and Travancore join to become the state of Kerala

1961 End of Portuguese colonial rule in Goa

1973 Merging of Coorg and the states of Bombay, Madras and Hyderabad into present-day Karnataka

2004 The Sikh Dr. Manmohan Singh is voted India's first non-Hindu prime minister

Red-hot chilli peppers: without them, spicy South Indian cuisine is nothing

Whatever your particular priorities might be, Goa and Karnataka, Kerala and Tamil Nadu have more than enough variety, and all year round as well. High season in Goa is considered to be October, the start of the dry season, which goes on to May/June.

But if you've ever seen the film 'Monsoon Wedding', you'll know how romantic a warm tropical downpour can be. Many beach hotels offer special monsoon deals. Anyway, it hardly ever pours down the entire day, heavy showers alternat-

> **Every visitor succumbs to the shopping**

ing with sunny spells, and certainly anyone who is interested in experiencing India without all the foreign tourists, wants to get to know the locals better, and would like to sample the slightly melancholic mood, should come during the monsoon. But that's India for intermediates or advanced.

2010 Rampant corruption is the dominant domestic issue

2011 1.21 billion people live in India, 181 million more than at the previous census in 2001

2012 Ex-Finance Minister Pranab Mukherjee becomes the 13th President of India. As head of state he replaces Pratibha Devisingh Patil; he is considered a supporter of Sonia Gandhi (daughter-in-law of Indira Gandhi), chairperson of the United Progressive Alliance

WHAT'S HOT

1 Funky sounds

Music When long queues start to form outside a music venue like the *Unwind Café (8, Manikesh Wari Rd, Kilpauk, Chennai)*, it is likely that an indie band is playing. India's heart beats to rocking, funky sounds, like those of Chennai's *Junkyard Groove (www.facebook.com/junkyardgroove, photo)* or the metal band *Dhwesha (www.reverb nation.com/dhwesha)*, who sing in the regional Kannada language. In Bengaluru the *Landmark* book and record store is another focal point for indie concerts *(in the Forum, 21, Hosur Rd)*.

Across town

2

Parkour Bollywood star Akshay Kumar *(www.aksh aykumar.org)* has made this form of urban acrobatics trendy throughout the country. Since the actor began negotiating obstacles in his films, the courses given by Ashwin Mohan have enjoyed great popularity *(3, Curley Street, Bengaluru, photo)* and the parkour group *Chennai Ninjas (www.chennaiparkour.com)* has been recruiting lots of new members. You can buy the correct outfit from *Sports'n'Style (11, Uttaradi Mutt Rd, Bengaluru)*.

Community input

3

Art Little wonder that artists in Bengaluru, the city of the internet, draw on ideas inspired by the masses. Just like Meenu Jaipura, who involves her workshop participants in the creative process *(in the Mahua Art Gallery, 161 Rajmahal Vilas)*. Also Lalitha Shankar *(www. lalithashankar.com)* uses the thoughts and ideas of her customers for her installations. Amongst other places you can see the results at branches of the *Sumukha* gallery in Bengaluru and Chennai *(187, St. Mary's Rd, Alwarpet, photo)*.

Urban farmers

Green fingers It isn't just Bengaluru's Botanic Gardens that are worth a visit. On request, some private residents will let you have a look at their roof gardens; urban gardening is now very fashionable in India's big cities. Bloggers and websites such as *www.theyoungfarmer.com* deal with topics involving choice of seed and fertiliser, but there are also courses and even school lessons on the subject *(photo)*. The author Dr. B. N. Viswanath and his *Garden City Farmers (enquiries tel. 94486 2 95 28)* in Bengaluru organise one-day workshops. It's not just about designing beautiful flowerbeds but also about creating a sustainable future and making a stand against environmental pollution. In Chennai you can also join plant-themed walks.

Stylish jewellery

East meets west Indian women are known for their beautiful jewellery, pieces in which every stone and every shape has a meaning. This is something that contemporary jewellery designers have not forgotten – though the main focus of their work is on fashion. They create dangly earrings, necklaces and bracelets that would make heads turn even on the streets of London or New York. But the items still have the typical look of the subcontinent. Good places to go include *Gehna (2, Casa Major Rd, Egmore)* and *Amrapali (near Amethyst 2/11, Kasturi Estate, 3rd Street)* in Chennai or the traditional jeweller *Ganjam (148, Embassy Square, Infantry Rd, Bengaluru)* as well as a branch of *Anmol (www.anmoljewellers.in, photo)*.

IN A NUTSHELL

BEAUTY

Visiting an Indian beauty parlour is a wonderful experience and, even if hygiene standards away from the good hotels leave something to be desired, the traditional applications are unmatched. You could easily spend a whole day there, having a facial with purely herbal ingredients, an epilation using the ancient threading method, and enjoying a relaxing head, body or foot massage. Henna is not just used as a dye but also as a healthy hair pack, enriched with yoghurt, egg, lemon and scented oils. The treatments cost a fraction of what you would pay in western Europe. So even in the less salubrious establishments, you'll probably be quite happy to close your eyes.

CASTE SYSTEM

The caste system was first mentioned in sacred texts *(veda)* as long ago as 1200 BC. Officially, since the adoption of the modern constitution in 1950, it has been abolished, but it still exists in the minds of many Indians. For example, they find it unthinkable to have a marriage between people of a different caste. Even today, a person's social background can be determined from their family name, which provides information on former status. The caste system consists of four main castes *(varnas)*, which are further divided into many sub-groups or *jatis*. Brahmins, traditionally the spiritual and intellectual elite, the priests and interpreters of holy scripts, occupy the highest-ranking varna. The second-high-

Photo: Fishing boats on the beach in front of the mosque in Kovalam

Between poverty and riches: stark contrasts characterise the south of the world's most populous democracy

est caste is that of the *kshatryas,* made up of warriors, princes and high officials. Traders and farmers were the *vaishas*, while the *shudras* included labourers, tenant farmers and slaves. Forming a special caste of their own were the *parias* or *dalits* – the Untouchables. They were, for example, denied access to the temple and couldn't even cast their shadow on the food of someone belonging to a higher caste.

ECONOMY

India's economy is booming. With a growth rate of 8% in the 2011–12 financial year, India is the world's fastest growing economy after China. In terms of GDP, by the middle of this century it is expected to lie in third place after China and the USA. India already plays a major role in the global market, deriving much of its strength from the IT industry.

And yet it is still the case that despite the emergence of a burgeoning middle class, there is nowhere else with such a large gap between rich and poor. The subcontinent might have the world's largest number of millionaires and billionaires, but the average annual per capita in-

Equal rights? Not in the countryside

come is just 725 US\$. An astonishing 28 percent of the population lives below the poverty line of 1 US\$ per day, preserving India's status as a developing country.

ENVIRONMENT

Several resort hotels, not just the *cgh earth group* that has been at the fore-front of developments in ecotourism and sustainability but smaller resorts as well, have developed a high degree of environmental awareness. It will look spotless too at other accommodation, including the stretches of beach that belong to them. But as soon as you leave the clean zone, it's over with the environmental awareness. Plastic bottles and bags litter the ground, and no one feels the need to get rid of them. Survival is more important than refuse disposal, they say. But there is hope. Jose Dominic, founding member of the *Ecotourism Society of India,* works in the field of public awareness. His society organises presentations all over the country, because it's clear that rubbish isn't just a problem for local people but it also represents a threat to the tourist industry. According to its director, the emphasis of the ecotourism initiative is on sustainability. Its aim is to involve the inhabitants of the different areas, so that they too benefit from tourism. And then people will start to think about how waste could be converted into electricity. There are also problems in the Backwaters of Kerala, where villagers do their washing with lots of detergent and also throw their rubbish in the channels. 'We want to increase awareness of the need for a clean environment there as well, but for houseboats there's already a law against the disposing of waste in the water,' says Dominic.

FASHION

The Asia look is in. Glittering bangles for your wrist, bags with pictures of Indian gods, colourful, beaded slippers and embroidered tunics, these are all must-haves for fashion conscious ladies. At parties in Goa, guests even wear costumes that look like they're straight out of Bollywood movies. Indian fashion designers have long since risen through the ranks of European labels. Sabyasachi Mukherjee, who designs under the *Sabyasachi* label, shows off his creations during New York Fashion Week and is promoted by Sotheby's as a top fashion designer. But cheap hippie-style clothes are also very popular. In the resorts of Kovalam and Varkala, at the Anjuna fleamarket and at Ingo's Night Market between Baga and Anjuna in Goa, multi-coloured cotton and silk skirts flap in the breeze, as do wide, often wrapped-round trousers that are incredibly convenient for travelling. Then there are cashmere sweaters from Nepal and colourful cardigans from Tibet. Another tip for female tourists who would like to wear a sari during their trip to India is to make sure an Indian woman shows you how to 'wrap' it correctly; otherwise, the folds won't fall in the right places and the triangle at the back will be too low. And that would look ridiculous! More practical and every bit as exotic is the *salwar kameez*, a pair of narrow trousers with a matching knee-length tunic.

FILM INDUSTRY

Bollywood in Mumbai (Bombay) is well-known; the fact that there is also a Kollywood, less so. It is based in Chennai (Madras) in Tamil Nadu and ever since 1916 it has been producing films that are mainly in the Tamil language, with the first Tamil talkie coming out in 1931. The name is derived from the Hindi film industry from Mumbai and the district in Chennai – Kodanbakkan – where the studios are located. Kollywood films, however, tend to focus on action and martial arts rather than on Bollywood-style love scenes, which is partly why they are so big in Japan. Among the most successful actors of Tamil film was Marudur Gopalamenon Ramachandran, who later became prime minister of Tamil Nadu. And the current prime minister of the state, Dr. Kalaignar Karunanidhi, once wrote movie scripts.

LANGUAGES

Because each state has its own language with many different dialects, some even with different written forms, Hindi was designated as India's official language. Due to colonial history, the second official language is English, which is spoken mainly by the elite but also by increasing numbers of the burgeoning middle class who need to communicate internationally. As far as the main local languages of South India are concerned, *Konkani* is spoken in Goa, *Kannada* in Karnataka, the very quick-fire *Malayalam* in Kerala and *Tamil* in Tamil Nadu.

MUSIC

Forming the basis of classical Indian music is the *raga,* a basic melodic structure. The Sanskrit word translates as feeling or mood. So through its particular melody and range of tonal nuances, each raga conjures up a different mood. Similar to jazz, the musician has a lot of scope for improvisation. The versatile *sitar* often serves as the main instrument, while the rhythm is determined by the two-drum *tabla*. While classical music is often difficult for Western ears to grasp, the songs and dance music from Bollywood movies are currently very popular. Indian pop music is substantially influenced by the musical genre known as *bhangra*, which originates from the Punjab. You can hear bhangra in many Bollywood soundtracks. Thus, with the song *Mundian To Bach Ke* ('Beware of the Boys') by *Panjabi MC* took the European charts by storm. It even occupied the top spot in Italy. Mixed with house and reggae, bhangra is now an established part of the club scene in South Asia.

POPULATION AND POLITICS

At the last census in 2011, 1.21 billion people were recorded as living in India. The population had risen by 181 million from the time of the previous census in 2001. That makes India the world's most populous parliamentary democracy. The named in their respective local languages. Some names such as Chennai – the former Madras – bear no resemblance to their old name; others, such as Udhagamandalam for Ooty and Thiruvananthapuram for Trivandrum, are so cumbersome, that even the inhabitants continue to use the old names. Since

Everyday beliefs: giving money to a sadhu, a holy man, will boost your karma

enormous country is made up of 28 states and seven union territories including in the south Puducherry, the Andaman and Nicobar Islands and Lakshadweep. Its capital is New Delhi. In contrast to the federal states, each with its own local government, the union territories are subject to direct control fom the government in New Delhi. In order to erase the last vestiges of colonialism, since the mid-1990s many cities have been re-

2004, the ruling Congress Party together with eleven other parties has formed the coalition of the United Progressive Alliance (UPA), which governs India. The prime minister is Dr. Manmohan Singh; the head of state is the lawyer and former finance minister Pranab Mukherjee.

SPIRITUALITY

In India, faith and superstition merge together. Every practising Hindu

goes to the temple to pray at least twice a day. And even enlightened business-men will consult the 'house astrologer' before closing a deal to check that the timing is auspicious. Spirituality in India has a tradition stretching back more than 3000 years. Even today, through the doc-trine of karma, it provides the poorest of the poor with the hope of better fortune in the next life. An ashram (literally: place of religious retreat) is a centre of contemplation, visited by disciples of a particular master, or guru. Depending on his individual philosophy he will lead his followers on a journey of spiritual and religious discovery, often aided by medi-tation and yoga. Sri Sathya Sai Baba (1926–2011) was revered even more strongly than a guru, namely as an *Ava-tar* – an incarnation of God. His ashrams in Puttaparthi/Andra Pradesh and in Whitefield/Karnataka still enjoy great popularity. His credo was: all religions are equally important.

Known simply as 'Amma', Sri Mata Amri-tanandamayi was born in 1953 in Kerala and her ashram is located in the fishing village of Amrita. Always compassionate and caring towards everyone, she blesses those in search of healing and truth with a hug – worldwide she has now hugged more than 24 million people. Mother Meera was born in 1960 in Andra Pradesh, but now lives in Germany and on her travels there and abroad she blesses her followers with a touch on the temple.

TSUNAMI

The tsunami unleashed by the Indi-an Ocean earthquake on 26 December 2004 caused massive damage in South India. Thousands of people died along the coast and thousands more, notably fishermen, lost their livelihoods. Of the official Indian death toll of around 11,000, some 7800 were from the state of Tamil Nadu. Worst hit was the district of Nagapattinam, where the waves reached a height of about 6m (20ft). Studies from South India show that in areas where mangrove forests and other natural barriers were still relatively in-tact and the statutory coastal protection zone of 500m was observed, hardly any people or buildings came to harm. To-day, virtually all traces of the tsunami have been removed, though many of the affected fishermen have still not re-ceived any compensation.

WOMEN

It is quite a balancing act for In-dian women to move between moder-nity and tradition. In the cities of South India, most young women now have a job or profession. Thanks to their finan-cial independence, they also have much more self-confidence than just a few decades ago. In rural areas, however, the situation looks very different. Here, girls have far fewer educational oppor-tunities. While the constitution guaran-tees them equal rights with men, this is hardly apparent in everyday life. In rural society, the woman is still largely subor-dinate. Except in Goa, where young women can freely choose whom they want to marry, it is mainly still the par-ents who select a suitable match for their daughter in an arranged marriage. In the world of politics, by contrast, the transformation started in the days of Indira Gandhi, who was prime minister of India from 1966 to 1977 and again from 1980 to 1984. Since then, further important political posts have been filled by women. Between 2007 and 2012, for example, Prathiba Devisingh Patil was, as president, India's head of state.

FOOD & DRINK

Generally speaking South Indian cuisine is much hotter than northern Indian. Coconut is a ubiquitous ingredient: it is present in many sauces, is used for its oil and even appears in the form of alcohol, like *toddy* (palm wine) and *arrack* (a strong spirit).

The signature dish is *thali,* which consists of a mound of rice, up to 36 different vegetarian delights piled up in appetizing little heaps and traditionally served on a banana leaf. In Kerala this lavish dish is called *sadya*. It tastes best when you eat with your fingers (only with the right 'clean' hand), as is the norm in India. Hotel restaurants now serve up streamlined versions on a plate. However, when eaten from a banana leaf the taste is incomparably better, and of course

more authentic. Freshly caught *king prawns* and *lobster* from the sea are prepared in a variety of ways. Rice is the most important staple in South India. It is not only used as a grain but also as flour. Popular dishes include *biryani,* mixed rice dishes with vegetables and usually also meat. Curries *(karis)* originate from Tamil cuisine. The special taste is achieved by the use of specific mixtures of spices. These include curry leaves, tamarind, coriander, ginger, garlic, chillies, cinnamon, cloves, cardamom, cumin, fennel, aniseed, fenugreek seeds, nutmeg, coconut, turmeric and rose water. It has nothing much in common with the curry powder used in Europe.

The best breakfast in India – both in terms of taste and health – can be en-

Photo: Chicken curries

A treat for the taste buds: in the south of India every dish, every bite reveals another sensory experience

joyed in Kerala. One speciality available all across India is the *dosa,* very thinly rolled rice flour pancakes, which are served with coconut chutney and spicy sambar sauce. While Kerala is renowned for having India's best seafood, Goan menus offer a variety of chicken dishes, unusual puddings and of course seafood specialities such as prawn curry. The native Goans learned how to prepare spicy sausage from the Portuguese. *Vindaloo* is derived from the Portuguese 'carne em vinha d'alhos', meat marinated in wine

and garlic. The addition of red chillies and spices make the dish especially hot. South India's most sophisticated cuisine is prepared in the region of Chettinad in Tamil Nadu, which in addition to typical Tamil elements, also combines influences from Burma, Indonesia and Europe. Be that as it may, young chefs are putting increasing emphasis on light cuisine. Desserts are often sugar- and fat-free, and made from cereals, fruit and lentils. India is a fun place to travel for vegetarians. Because millions of Indians live

LOCAL SPECIALITIES

▶ **appam** – simple rice pancakes

▶ **bhaji** – vegetables fried in a batter of gram flour

▶ **chicken cafrial** – diced chicken coated with a spicy sauce, a Goan speciality

▶ **chourisso** – red-coloured sausages in Goa

▶ **chutney (chatni)** – spicy to hot paste made of pickled fruit or vegetables and served with thalis

▶ **dhal** – red lentils

▶ **feni** – a spirit made from cashew nuts

▶ **garam masala** – take care: a very hot mixture of spices

▶ **idiyappam** – made from rice flour and served for breakfast with a hot vegetable sauce (photo right)

▶ **idli sambar** – flat rice cake with a spicy sauce

▶ **jaggery** – these brown lumps made from sugar cane are much healthier than sugar, contain many minerals, proteins and vitamins and are also used in Ayurvedic cuisine

▶ **kerala parippu** – really a runny curry made of dhal, desiccated coconut, green and red chillies as well as ghee (clarified butter)

▶ **kurlleachi karti** – crabmeat curry with dessicated coconut

▶ **masala** – spice mixture for vegetables, dosas, salads and rice

▶ **murg masala** – chicken with spices, nuts and yoghurt

▶ **pakora** – vegetables or egg fried in batter

▶ **panir** – unsalted white cheese cut into cubes

▶ **pappadam** – thin cracker made from rice or lentil flour and fried in oil until crisp

▶ **pilau** – spiced rice with vegetables

▶ **puttu** – solid mound of rice flour and coconut, usually served for breakfast

▶ **rasam** – spicy hot soup, usually made from tomatoes

▶ **roti** – flat bread made from wheat, oats, millet or corn flour, so excellent for soaking up the sauces

▶ **sambar** – slightly runny side dish made from vegetables, lentils, chillies and tamarind

▶ **samosa** – deep-fried pastry parcel usually filled with potato and peas but also with meat

▶ **tandoori** – chicken or other meat prepared in a cylindrical clay oven (photo left)

▶ **thali** – different dishes presented in small bowls – or on a banana leaf in Kerala

▶ **uppama** – braised vegetables

without meat, the vegetarian cuisine is among the most varied and diverse in the world. For practising Hindus purity of mind and spirit also means abstinence from meat, fish, poultry, and often eggs as well. In every city, in every village there are several vegetarian restaurants. And every 'normal' *(non-veg)* restaurant either has a separate menu, if not a separate seating area or dining room for vegetarians. Those who can't tolerate hot and spicy food should ask for 'non spicy'.

The safest beverage is the refreshing juice of the *king coconut* – the young coconut. If you really want to be sure, you can bring along your own straw for drinking at the street stalls. Drinking soda with lemon juice and salt is a good way to combat salt loss. The same goes for *lassi* – whipped yogurt, often served with fruit, like mango lassi for example. Beers such as *Kingfisher* and *Golden Eagle* are brewed in India; they generally have a lower alcohol content than European beers. The Portuguese introduced wine to Goa as long ago as the 16th century, but in recent years India has made a name for itself cultivating its own vines. Experts speak of India's 'vine-growing triangle', which covers the regions of Nashik, Pune and Mumbai in Maharashtra. As far as quantity is concerned, this still doesn't match internationally-renowned wine-producing areas, but the quality can easily compete, with Indian Merlot, Sauvignon and Chardonnay receiving high praise at wine fairs. Because the state now promotes this economic sector and has introduced the appropriate tax breaks, it is expected that Indian wine production will experience continued growth. Even now, many wineries organise tastings.

Tea is served at every opportunity. Because it is brewed strongly, it is drunk with milk. Coffee, too, is popular, and tastes great when made from locally produced, freshly roasted beans.

Thali, a synonym for variety

As a rule, you shouldn't touch anything that you can't cook or peel. Otherwise your holiday might be ruined by long-term gastric problems. Only drink water from bottles, and check first that the cap is really sealed. Even filtered water, which stands in jugs on restaurant tables, is often not pure enough for western constitutions. Buying ice cream from a beach vendor is an absolute no-no.

SHOPPING

Don't pack your suitcase to the brim otherwise it'll be overflowing for the journey home. Most holidaymakers end up having to buy an additional bag on the spot in order to get all those beautiful things back. Immerse yourself in the bustling world of markets and bazaars, but don't forget to haggle. After the trader names his price, you name yours – about half the amount. If you stick to your guns, you can usually meet somewhere in the middle. You should never respond to offers from beach vendors with a blunt 'No'. It's better to say 'maybe tomorrow'. That way there's no loss of face on either side. In the state-run emporia there are fixed prices – in contrast to the many cashmere shops, which often call themselves an emporium. Take care when purchasing antiques. There are some excellent forgers who can make furniture and coins look old. And besides you aren't allowed to take anything out of the country that's more than 100 years old.

Tailors will happily make up garments for you, such as a shirt or a *salwar kameez*, a long blouse with tapering trousers. It will take a couple of hours at most, and the price is very reasonable. The same goes for western cuts, which any Indian tailor will be able to copy for you.

JEWELLERY

The shops sell some beautiful gold and silver jewellery, but the gold often has a distinctive reddish tinge. Have the dealer show you a certificate of authenticity, and if you want to play safe only buy at jewellery shops that are identified as 'government approved'. Silver is very beautifully worked and often decorated with semi-precious stones. A common 'stone' is rich golden-yellow *amber*. Glittering *bangles* have also become popular in the West – whether with stones or without, real or fake. Several are stacked on one arm, blending complimentary colours, tones and textures. In India, fashion jewellery is available everywhere from the so-called *ladies' shops*, which can often just be small kiosks.

LEATHER GOODS

Only the very elegant shopping centres, such as in Bengaluru, will sell suitcases or briefcases that conform to European tastes. Most models qualify as 'exotic' at best. That also applies to the strap sandals that are available everywhere. But there are very nice belts and wallets and all manner of etui bags.

Shop till you drop: silk, jewellery, spices –
it's one big consumer paradise at the
markets and in the bazaars and stores

PASHMINA SHAWLS

South India has lots of cashmere shops, which sell carpets, jewellery and hundreds of pashmina shawls in every imaginable colour and design. The quality varies considerably, a shawl costing anything between £10 and £500. Genuine shawls are made out of cashmere wool, the hair of the Himalayan mountain goat, which is five times finer than a human hair. The best quality comes from the hair under the chin of the goat, and clearly such items are going to cost a lot more than just a few pounds. As proof of the fine structure of genuine cashmere shawls, dealers will often pull them through a finger ring.

SILK AND COTTON

India's best silk comes from Mysore and Madurai. Quality ranges from ultra fine to heavy duty. Even if you don't want to wear a sari yourself, the material, between 4m and 8m long and 1.2m wide, will come in handy as a sofa or bed cover, or even as a curtain. You can have pretty cushion covers made up from the broad brocade borders, usually on the spot. Cotton comes in wonderful designs; South Indian dealers import beautiful materials in authentic colours from Gujarat, where the dyes are fixed in a salt lake.

SPICES

Saffron is one of the world's most expensive spices – but it's affordable in India, particularly in places such as the spice yards of Fort Cochin in Kerala. In the markets there are cones piled high with cardamom, ginger, turmeric, vanilla, etc.; select the amount you require and the trader will pack it for you.

THE PERFECT ROUTE

TEMPLE, TEMPLE, TEMPLE

① *Chennai* → p. 96 is the perfect starting point. Here you can hire a car with driver for the entire journey, or arrange to cover some sections by train. Before setting off from Chennai, climb the 106 steps to the white *San Thome Basilica,* where tradition states that St Thomas the Apostle met his martyrdom. The East Coast Road follows the sea south to **②** *Mamallapuram* → p. 103 (photo left). At this unique Unesco World Heritage Site allow yourself plenty of time to admire the *sea temples* and the nine *cave temples* with reliefs full of elephants and celestial beings. The journey continues southwards to **③** *Thanjavur* → p. 108, which has all of 90 temples. You can enjoy a superb view over **④** *Tiruchirappalli* → p. 109 from the 83-m (272-ft) high *Rock Fort* crowned by the *Ucchi Pillar Temple.* Just 6km (4mi) away, the legendary temple city of **⑤** *Srirangam* → p. 110 lies on an island between two rivers, its bazaars thronging with pilgrims. South India's greatest marvel, however, is in **⑥** *Madurai* → p. 105 – the *Sri Meenakshi Sundareshwarar Temple,* festooned with some 33 million figures of gods and demons. Before the visit you can order a garment from one of the 250 tailors in the adjacent bazaar, and pick it up afterwards.

TIGERS, TEA AND PARADISE BEACHES

Now it's up into the hills with their tea gardens and into the **⑦** *Periyar National Park* → p. 58 (photo right). Whether you're on a boat trip, trekking or bamboo rafting, elephants and monkeys will be likely to cross your path and, with a bit of luck, even a tiger. Afterwards you can go to the beach, namely the one at **⑧** *Varkala* → p. 68. Climb the steps to the top of the red cliffs, and enjoy the views from one of the many open-air cafés, bars or restaurants. Even if it's only for a few hours, in **⑨** *Alappuzha* → p. 55, the Venice of the East, you should board a houseboat made of bamboo and coconut and take a relaxing journey along the enchanted *Backwaters.* In **⑩** *Kochi* → p. 49 immerse yourself in the bustle of the Old Town's narrow alleyways; at sunset take a boat trip to photograph the *Chinese fishing nets.*

PARTIES, SHOPPING, ANCIENT SPLENDOUR

⑪ *Mysore* → p. 91 is the fairytale city of the Maharajas. During festivals the magnificent palace of *Amba Vilas* is illuminated by 96,000 light bulbs. On then to the shopper's paradise of ⑫ *Bangalore → p.76*: silk, saris, jewellery and rugs – along the MG Road there is one fantastic shop after another. This western-influenced city with its plentiful nightlife is also often called the *Pub City*.

EROTICA IN STONE

Quite a sight. The erotic depictions at the *Hoysala Temple* in ⑬ *Belur → p.89* are extremely detailed. An almost mystical scene unfolds at ⑭ *Hampi → p.80*. The location alone, between granite rocks and the river, is stunning. Hire a bicycle to explore the extensive complex – also a Unesco World Heritage Site – with its temples, palaces and the famous Stone Chariot. Four cave temples are hidden among the red sandstone hills of ⑮ *Badami → p.85*. In the first one you can take lessons from the 18-armed statue of Nataraja (Shiva), who demonstrates 81 different dance moves.

SWIMMING, PARTYING, RIVER TRIP UNDER THE STARS

Now you can relax on the endless beaches of Goa. This, the smallest Indian state, is strongly influenced by its Portuguese heritage and exudes joie de vivre. The Queen of the sands is considered to be ⑯ *Calangute Beach → p.35*. But you should also definitely visit ⑰ *Old Goa (Velha Goa) → p.43*, with its snow-white church *Basilica Bom Jesus*. And finally, at sunset treat yourself to a romantic boat trip on the *Mandovi River* in the capital of Goa, ⑱ *Panaji → p.40*. Return to Chennai from Dambolim airport.

2635 km/1637 mi. Driving time: 49 hrs. Recommended duration: 16–20 days Detailed map of the route in the road atlas, the pull-out map and on the back cover

GOA

In their search for spices and silk, Portuguese traders landed in Goa in 1510. They were so taken with this fertile region that they stayed for 451 years. Goa only gained independence from Portugal in 1961; in 1987 it became India's 25th state. With colourful Hindu temples standing next to whitewashed churches, the inhabitants here have a more relaxed outlook on life than in the north. The great thing about Goa is the blend; colonial charm mixed with Indian mysticism, bustling markets and exotic fragrances. Many things here are called by their Portuguese names, and some of the older generation can still speak the language of the former colonial masters, who have also left behind their fortresses, their mansions, their food, their beliefs and their culture. With an area of 1429 sq. mi, this is India's smallest state. At the foot of the Western Ghats mountain range, green rice fields alternate with dense palm groves. In the settlements fringing the paddies time seems to have stood still and picturesque villages such as *Canacona taluka* near Margao appear almost untouched by civilisation.

But Goa's biggest attraction is undoubtedly the endless broad beaches that run the length of the 101-km (63-mi) Konkan Coast, interrupted only by river estuaries. Generally speaking the beaches in the north are livelier than those of the south. Most of them have long-since been abandoned by the hippies, who nowadays tend to congregate in the far north and far south. In the evening the lively beaches with all their activities are transformed into romantic locations, with

Photo: Palolem Beach

Paradise beaches and the Portuguese lifestyle: the seaside plays a big part in India's smallest state

many restaurants setting up chairs and tables on the beach. Sitting under a starry sky, your feet in the sand and the sound of breaking waves in the background – that is the ultimate Goa experience.

CALANGUTE-BAGA

(140 A5) (*□ B6*) Once small fishing villages, the two resorts of Calangute (*koli gutti* = land of the fisherman) and Baga have grown together almost seamlessly (pop. 17,000).

The double community is now a hive of activity. Calangute-Baga makes an ideal base for tours into the area north of the Mandovi River.

ST ALEX CHURCH

The two towers and dome of the snow-white St Alex Church in Calangute are visible from afar. Built more than 400 years ago, this pretty church is one of the oldest in Goa. Inside, one of the highlights is the magnificent altar. *Chogm Rd*

smaller scale. There are cruises of varying lengths. The 2-day tour aboard a double-decker, for example, departs Chapora/Siolim at 3pm, arriving in time to

Well maintained: even after 400 years St Alex still gleams snow white

FOOD & DRINK

O PESCADOR RESTAURANT & BAR
This large open-air restaurant with seating for around 100 enjoys a good reputation for its excellent fish and seafood dishes. A live band plays on weekends. *From 6pm | Baga Rd, Cobra Vaddo, Calangute | tel. 0832 2 27 94 47 | Moderate*

SHOPPING

ACRON ARCADE
In the neighbouring town of Candolim there are two different fashion outlets for Indian designers. You'll also find books, CDs and DVDs. *Oct–April daily 10am–10pm, May–Sept 10am–8pm | 283 Ft Aguada Rd | www.acronarcade.com*

SPORTS & ACTIVITIES

HOUSEBOAT TOURS
Like Kerala, Goa offers houseboat cruises along its backwaters, albeit on a much

watch the sunset over the mangroves. *Nov–April | 14000 Rs | Johns Boat Tours | tel. 0832 6 52 01 90 | www.johnboattours.com*

BEACHES IN THE VICINITY

From north to south, all **(140 A5)** *(ꄰ B6)*

VAGATOR
This beach at the foot of Chapora Fort consists of two sections, separated by a rocky headland. The northern part, *Ozram*, is smaller and more popular, the southern, *Big Vagator* is more secluded. Generally, Vagator attracts a smarter, younger crowd than Anjuna.

ANJUNA
Cows, ageing hippies and package tourists share the warm sands of Anjuna. At full moon, wild rave parties are held between the palm trees and the rocks.

GOA

CALANGUTE ⭐

The 'Queen of the Beaches' extends for more than 8km (5mi) from Fort Aguada to the small river estuary at *Baga Beach*. Essentially, Baga, Calangute, Candolim and Sinquerim constitute different sections of what is one very long beach, each having its own character. The Calangute section is lined with fast food and massage stalls. Designed in Portuguese style, the *Ronil Beach Hotel (Baga, Saunta-vaddo | tel. 0832 2 27 61 01 | Moderate)* complex has 126 rooms and two pools.

CANDOLIM

This busy beach is lined with shacks and bars. One nice restaurant is the *Palm & Sands*, which serves Goan, Chinese and European cuisine. Speciality: *apple pie (Dando | tel. 0832 2 47 91 71 | Budget)*.

SINQUERIM

This narrow continuation of Candolim beach extends for 800m as far as the Fort Aguada headland. Lots of water sports are on offer. Accommodation options include the colonial-style *Aldeia Santa Rita (55 rooms | Sinquerim, Candolim | tel. 0832 2 47 98 68 | Moderate)* where 11 villas surround a pool.

ENTERTAINMENT

TITO'S

This is a famous nightclub, dating from the hippy era. The party began in 1971 and is still going on today. It's on the go 365 days a year – each day having a fresh theme. *Tito's Lane Baga*

WHERE TO STAY

ATMAN ECO ART RESORT ☺

Behind the sand dunes of Pernem, the northernmost taluka in Goa, are these eco huts made of bamboo and wood and beautifully decorated and furnished with natural materials by an Italian-Indian couple. In the rooftop restaurant *Sole e Luna* they serve Italian cuisine made from regional produce. *Dando Village, Gircarwada, Arambol | Pernem | tel. 0988 13116 43 | www.atmangoa.com | Budget*

MARCO POLO HIGHLIGHTS

CASA DE GOA
Here you will find 12 Mediterranean-style villas grouped around a pool. *50 rooms | Calangute | tel. 0832 227999 | www. casadegoa.com | Moderate–Expensive*

D'MELLOS GUESTHOUSE 🌿
This cosy guesthouse run by Peter d'Mello sits in its own tropical garden between Candolim and Calangute. The 300-m long stretch of beach is almost deserted. It has its own beach restaurant and almost all of the 20 balconied rooms have an ocean view. Internet café. *Escrivao Vaddo | Candolim, Bardez | tel. 0832 2 48 96 50 | www.dmellos.com | Budget*

PAES PEARL BEACH VILLA 🌿
Lying just 100m from Baga Beach, this old Goan-style house has been completely renovated. It has four spacious rooms with sea view and a small balcony. *Tel. 0982 2 17 56 92 | paespearl@gmail.com | Moderate*

INSIDER TIP ▶ YOGAMAGIC RESORT ☺
This eco resort consists of a main building with two suites and seven tents designed in oriental style. Its situation, adjacent to a rice paddy and stream, makes it a very relaxing place, together with the yoga and Ayurveda they offer. The resort uses solar energy and recyclable materials and composts its waste. *1586/1 Grand Chinvar | Vagator, Anjuna, Bardez | tel. 0832 6 52 37 96 | www.yogamagic.net | Moderate*

INFORMATION

TOURIST OFFICE CALANGUTE
Calangute Residency | Calangute Beach | tel. 0832 2 27 60 24

WHERE TO GO

ANJUNA FLEA MARKET ★
(140 A5) (*ϕ B6*)
In the 1970s travellers established this flea market at the end of the long Anjuna beach. Today, with its stalls full of crafts from Tibet, Nepal and Kashmir, colourful clothes and tattoo artists, it is considered one of Goa's main attractions. *Wed 11am to sunset | 2.5km (1.5mi) north of the end of the beach*

INSIDER TIP ▶ ARPORA SATURDAY NIGHT BAZAAR (140 A5) (*ϕ B6*)
In neighbouring Arpora the bazaar really livens up on Saturday evenings. In the middle of the market various artists take to the stage, and the surrounding stalls sell clothes, jewellery, spices and snacks. *7pm–midnight*

FORT AGUADA (140 A5) (*ϕ B6*)
Between 1609 and 1612, the Portuguese built the sprawling Fort Aguada on the headland at the end of Sinquerim beach. Within the citadel stands a white lighthouse; dating from 1846 it was the first lighthouse to be built in the whole of Asia. *4km (2.5mi) south*

MAPUSA (140 A5) (*ϕ B6*)
The market in Mapusa is held from Monday to Saturday. It's well worth visiting, especially on a Friday when farmers from northern Goa arrive with their fruit, vegetables, pottery, flowers and sweet bananas. *11km (7mi) northeast*

PALOLEM

(140 A5) (*ϕ B6*) **The entire taluka (district) of Canacona only has around 11,000 inhabitants. The lively little town of Palolem really just consists of one street, *Palolem Beach Road*.**

It is lined with shops selling trinkets, cafés and restaurants and is particularly popular with young travellers. Instead of smart hotels, eco resorts made of mud and bamboo are the order of the day here. The half-moon Palolem beach is also known as 'Paradise Beach'. Enclosed by rocky headlands it is backed by a dense palm forest. North of Palolem, Goa's finest beaches stretch away as far as Majorda.

Palolem. *Palolem Beach | tel. 096 73 50 19 12 | Budget–Moderate*

RESTAURANT SAN FRANCISCO
Located right on Palolem Beach, the open bamboo veranda is an ideal place to relax. They serve delicious and very reasonably priced Goan dishes; specialities include tiger prawns and chicken Xacuti with coconut sauce. *Palolem*

Practical: pretty bags for carrying home pretty gifts from the Anjuna flea market

SIGHTSEEING

SRI MALLIKARJUNA TEMPLE
This temple near the small village of Sristhal in the southernmost taluka of Canacona, some 3km (2mi) inland from Palolem, was built as long ago as the 16th century and is dedicated to an incarnation of Shiva. The temple contains the statues of more than 60 Hindu deities.

FOOD & DRINK

DROPADI BEACH RESTAURANT
Serving everything from lobster to lasagne to north Indian *tandoori,* this is considered one of the best restaurants in

Beach | tel. 091 58 05 72 01 | www.camp sanfrancisco.com | Budget

SHOPPING

BUTTERFLY BOOK SHOP
Good for saving on the luggage: if you buy a book here you can sell it back to them when you've finished, naturally for a lower price. Borrowing is also possible. Languages available range from English and German to Russian and Japanese. *Ward 14, Pundalik Gaitondi | www.yogavillapalolem.com*

SPORTS & ACTIVITIES

DOLPHIN WATCHING

Many of the fishermen on Palolem Beach are happy to take tourists out, either on fishing excursions or to go dolphin watching.

BEACHES IN THE VICINITY

All beaches from north to south (140 A5) (*∅ B6*)

MAJORDA, COLVA, BENAULIM, VARCA ★

Here, to the north of Palolem, is where numerous luxury resorts are located, including along the endless palm-lined beach that stretches from *Majorda* to *Varca*.

CAVELOSSIM, MOBOR, BETUL ★

This peaceful sandy beach, which has several sections, stretches north of Palolem as far as the tip of the promontory. The 5-star resort ☺ *The Leela Goa* (tel. 0832 2 87 12 34 | www.theleela.com |

Expensive) is regarded as the best hotel in the entire state. It lies between the Sal River and the peaceful Mabor Beach and has 206 rooms, six restaurants, a spacious spa with Ayurveda practitioner, a 12-hole golf course and tennis courts. The complex is run sustainably using solar power and rainwater for the gardens. On the banks of the Sal River is the open-air INSIDER TIP *Fisherman's Wharf* restaurant *(opposite the Holiday Inn, Cavelossim, Mobor | tel. 0832 2 87 13 17 | Moderate)*, which serves a variety of fish and seafood specialities. Also romantically situated on the Sal is the ☼ INSIDER TIP *River View (behind the Hotel Luisa | Cavelossim, Mobor | tel. 0832 2 87 18 98 | Budget)*, where both the seafood and the hotly spiced chicken are reasonably priced.

INSIDER TIP AGONDA

This 3-km (2-mi) long natural bay is framed by palms and casuarinas and lies some 5km (3mi) north of Palolem. The *Jardim a Mar (next to the church | Cavelossim | tel. 094 20 82 04 70 | www.*

On the beach of the Leela Goa resort there are still places under the palm trees

jardim-a-mar.com | Budget) offers accommodation in a total of 18 rooms, some in huts. They also offer yoga and Ayurveda, and from the ☼ open-air restaurant you can watch the leaping dolphins.

ENTERTAINMENT

PALOLEM BEACH PARTIES

The hub of local nightlife is the main Palolem beach. Every Saturday evening the British DJ Justin Mason runs his ● *Silent Noise Parties:* headphones can be set to a variety of music styles. *10pm–4am*

WHERE TO STAY

INSIDER TIP ▶ BHAKTI KUTIR ☺

The perfect place to unwind. This collection of 22 huts stands in a palm grove 200m above the south beach. The restaurant is mostly vegetarian. With its holistic philosophy, this lovely little resort also offers Ayurveda and yoga as well as meditation. Children can learn Hindi or Konkani, and cookery and music classes are also available. *296, Colomb | Palolem | tel. 0832 2 64 34 69 | www. bhaktikutir.com | Budget*

CAMP SAN FRANCISCO ☺

The Camp San Francisco is one of the best eco resorts. All of its 23 huts have shower and toilet. The best view is from the ☼ tree houses built on stilts right on the beach. *Just beyond Sea Shells Guest House along Palolem Road | tel. 091 58 05 72 01 | www.campsanfrancisco. com | Budget*

CIARAN'S CAMP ☺

Set in verdant grounds, twelve environmentally friendly beach huts made of coir (coconut husks), either with sea or garden view. No hut is further than 20m from the beach. The library has more than 1000 titles. To save on plastic, bottles are refilled with drinking water; they also have energy-saving light bulbs. Fresh seafood is served in the open-air beach restaurant. *Palolem Beach | tel. 0832 2 64 34 77 | www.ciarans.com | Budget*

INFORMATION

Information via the *Tourist Office* in *Margao town centre | tel. 0832 2 72 25 13*

WHERE TO GO

COTIGO WILDLIFE SANCTUARY (140 B6) (*ω B6*)

The 41-sq. mi. game park lies 10km (6mi) east of Palolem. Apes perform their acrobatics in the trees and, with a bit of luck, you'll be able to spot sloths, rhinos and leopards. From a 25-m (82-ft) high tower you can see animals drinking at a watering hole. Best time: Oct–March. *Daily 7.30am–5.30pm | Range Forest Office | www.goaforest.com*

MARGAO (140 A5) (*ω B6*)

Goa's second-largest city (pop. 78,000) has always been an important commercial centre, particularly when it comes to agricultural produce. Especially worth seeing therefore is the market, which extends from the main square as far as the old station. In the covered labyrinth full of colours, sounds and fragrances, you will find spices, clothes, pottery and handicrafts. For a special pampering experience try the ● *Millennium Beauty Parlour (QG 7, St Anthony Complex, next to St Sebastian's Church | Aquem Alto | tel. 098 22 48 28 64).* The owner Sarita Lobo does massages, manicures and pedicures, as well as facial treatments using mainly natural products. Goa's latest

At the Bragança estate in Chandor the daughter of the house leads you through the colonial past

fashion trends are available at *Boutique Blue – Clothes Bar (Coelho Apartments, Shop No. 1, opposite St Sebastian's Church | Aquem Alto | tel. 098 22 48 6136)*. Nelita Maurya, the owner, specialises in unusual Indo-European fusion fashion of silk, cotton, linen and chiffon with matching accessories. She also does made-to-measure garments. Crafts from all over India, made from environmentally friendly, mostly recycled materials, are available at the ⏱ *Tuk-Tuk-Shop (A 104, 1st floor, Pereira Plaza, opposite Hospicio Hospital)* and include baskets, books and writing paper processed from elephant dung. *30km (21mi) north*

PORTUGUESE HOUSES IN CHANDOR ★ (140 A5) (*🗺 B6*)

Original houses from Portuguese times, still occupied by the descendants of the people who built them, are open to visitors in Chandor. The *Bragança House* *(daily 9am–5.30pm | Rs 100 donation)* on Church Square is 450 years old in parts. Senhora Aurea Bragança Pereira displays the treasures of Goa's largest house: the magnificent ballroom with crystal chandeliers and typical Goan-style easy chairs. *Sara's Heritage House (Mon–Sat 9am–5pm | Fort Area, Cotta, Chandor)* is another such living museum. Sara Fernandes' pride and joy – apart from the salon – is the collection of old palanquins and temple statues. *35km (24mi) north*

PANAJI (PANJIM)

MAP INSIDE BACK COVER
(140 A5) (*🗺 B6*) Goa's capital (pop. 67,000) lies on the south bank of the broad estuary of the Mandovi River.

For several years the Nehru Bridge has linked Panaji to North Goa.

The city owes its charm to its wonderful location on the river as well as its many colonial buildings, churches, shady squares and green parks – particularly the Municipal Gardens.

SIGHTSEEING

CHURCH OF IMMACULATE CONCEPTION

Situated on the green central square of the Municipal Gardens and visible from afar is the *Church of Immaculate Conception.* There's a lovely view over Panaji from the hill, and the white Baroque church with its twin towers is the city's main landmark.

FOOD & DRINK

INSIDER TIP FULL MOON RESTAURANT

Freshly caught seafood and fish are served in the open-air restaurants on the beach. Romantic option: at the Full Moon restaurant have a table put right at the water's edge to enjoy dinner under the stars. *Bogmalo beach | tel. 0832 2 53 80 72 | Budget*

SHOPPING

The main shopping thoroughfare, *18th June Road*, runs from Church Square to Don Bosco's. Alongside the usual glamorous and glitzy sari shops, there are international designer outlets.

BEACHES IN THE VICINITY

All beaches, from north to south (140 A5) (*B6*)

DONA PAULA ★

Two kilometres (just over a mile) to the south of Miramar this glorious beach, framed by palms and casuarinas, has often served as a setting for Bollywood movies.

INSIDER TIP BOGMALO BAY

Bogmalo Bay is shaped like a sickle. Because of the calm water and the gently sloping beach, bathing is safe here all year round. The village of the same name consists of a church, Kashmir shops and tailors.

LOW BUDGET

▶ ● Motorcycle pilots transport their passengers to every destination at a fraction of the cost of a taxi and will wait patiently while you see the sights. Most drivers are also knowledgeable guides. You can find them everywhere in Goa at stands marked *Two Wheeler Taxi Stand. Rs 5/km*

▶ Several tailors have set up shop along the beach in Bogmalo Bay. Cheap and quick, they can easily copy items of clothing you take along, or will work from patterns in fashion magazines. The best in the trade is *Manolis (tel. 0832 2 53 8187).*

▶ Scooters, motorcycles and bicycles can be hired almost anywhere – there is no cheaper way of exploring Goa. Prices are between Rs 200 and Rs 400 per day. For scooters and motorcycles, make sure you bring along a copy of your driver's licence.

ENTERTAINMENT

INSIDER TIP CRUISING INTO THE SUNSET
Every day, in time for the sunset, boats head out from Panaji onto the Mandovi River. With live music, Goan dancing and dinner. Booking at the quayside.

WHERE TO STAY

BOGMALLO BEACH RESORT COTTAGES
Just 300m from the main hotel building, ☼ 15 beach cottages stand in their own palm tree garden, which overlooks Bogmalo Bay. All of them have a sea view and are equipped with veranda, bathroom and king-size bed. *Mormugao | tel. 0832 2538222 | www.bogmallo beachresort.com | Expensive*

CIDADE DE GOA
This luxury resort has 210 rooms, two pools and lies in park-like grounds just 7km (4mi) from Panaji on the 300-m long *Vainginim Beach*. The low-rise pink and ochre buildings have won several architectural awards. *Tel. 0832 2454545 | www.cidadedegoa.com | Expensive*

INSIDER TIP COCONUT CREEK RESORT
This magical little complex comprising ten pavilions and a pool lies hidden away in a palm grove in Bogmalo, 14km (9mi) from Panaji. Bogmalo Beach is just four minutes away. The 20 large rooms all have four-poster beds. *Tel. 0832 2538100 or 2538090 | joets@ sancharnet.in | Moderate*

DEVAAYA AND AYURVEDA & NATURE CURE CAMP
This extensive complex, with its total of 60 luxurious Goan-style rooms, nestles in lush greenery on Divar Island in the Mandovi River, so it's easy to focus on the Ayurveda treatments they have on offer. In addition: pool, tennis, basketball and yoga. *Tel. 0832 2280500 | www. devaaya.com | Moderate*

INFORMATION

GOA TOURISM DEVELOPMENT CORPORATION
Dr Alvares Costa Road | tel. 0832 24240013 | www.goa-tourism.com

TOURIST INFORMATION CENTER
Interstate Bus Terminus | tel. 0832 2225620

WHERE TO GO

GOA CHITRA ☺ (140 A5) (∅ B6)
This centre (approx. 35km/22mi south) is intended to portray the entire culture of Goa. A typical village has been constructed from used materials and an organic garden created. The museum includes displays of handicrafts and farming equipment. There's also an open-air theatre. *9am–6pm, last admission 5pm | admission RS 200 | St John the Baptist Church Rd, Mondo-Waddo | Benaulim | www.goachitra.com*

MOLEM & BHAGVAN MAHAVIR WILDLIFE SANCTUARY (140 B5) (∅ B6)
Goa shares this 93-sq. mi. national park at the foot of the Western Ghats with Maharashtra and Karnataka. The Goan part alone, the Molem National Park, covers an area of 41 sq. mi. The nearest town is Molem *(65km/40mi east)*. Residents of the park include leopards, elephants and bison. The best views are from the ☼ *Devil's Canyon* viewpoint, and the *Dudhsagar Falls* are truly spectacular. Jeep tours will take you into the heart of the jungle. *Daily 9am–5.30pm*

SAHAKARI SPICE FARM ★ ●
(140 A5) (📖 B6)

This spice farm is situated near Ponda on Highway 4A, 34km (21mi) southeast of Panaji. On a tour you will be able to touch and smell cloves, nutmeg, cardamom, cinnamon, ginger and vanilla. And a free massage is included. You can also take a ride on an elephant and help wash it in the river, and watch the crocodiles. *Daily 9.30am–4pm | RS 300 including organic lunch | tel. 0832 2 31 23 94 | www.sahakarifarms.com*

SRI MANGUESH TEMPLE
(140 A5) (📖 B6)

This temple stands in the small village of Priol, 28km (17mi) east of Panaji. Sri Manguesh is one of the many incarnations of Shiva, and a *lingam* – a phallus stone – is dedicated to him. The most striking feature of the famous Shiva shrine is its white, seven-storey oil lamp tower.

VELHA GOA ★ (140 A5) (📖 B6)

With its palaces, Baroque churches and mansions, the former capital of *Velha Goa* (pop. 5400), 10km (6mi) east of Panaji, is today a Unesco World Heritage Site. Hub of Portuguese colonial power until 1759, Old Goa is a relatively peaceful place today, situated on the Mandovi River. The most famous church in Goa is the *Basilica of Bom Jesus*, which contains the relics of Saint Francis Xavier, who came to Goa as a missionary in 1542 and died in China.

Dedicated to the god Shiva, the Sri Manguesh Temple with its seven-storey oil lamp tower

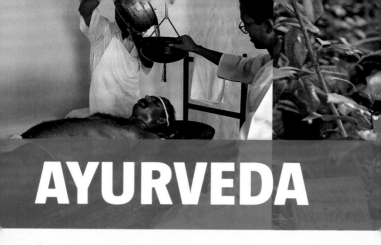

AYURVEDA

⭐ *Ayurveda* is the knowledge of life. *Ayur* means science, *veda* means life. The ancient art of healing has its origins in India and has been passed down by word of mouth since around 600 BC. According to its doctrine, illnesses are caused by an imbalance in the three *doshas* (bioenergies), *vata, pitta* and *kapha. Vata* (space and air) controls all movement, *pitta* (fire and some water) the metabolism, and *kapha* (earth and water) takes care of structure and stability. During the initial examination, the Ayurveda doctor will determine by various diagnostic techniques, which doshas have fallen out of balance and by how much. This will be followed by customised treatments and diets.

Sometimes the methods take a little getting used to, such as the 'steam bath', where only your head protrudes from a wooden box. Or the 'Kerala massage' with the therapist using his or her feet, holding on to a rope for balance. The four-handed synchronised massage, abhyangam, is held to be extremely relaxing, as is shirodhara the stress-reducing oil poured on the forehead. Authentic Ayurveda does not allow the consumption of fish or meat during the course of treatment; bathing is also taboo. The patient therefore has to be very self-disciplined on that paradise beach. To this end, meditation and yoga help promote harmony between body, spirit and soul. Ayurveda is claimed to work particularly well during the ● monsoon, because the pores in the skin are wide open enabling more effective treatment. A two-week cleansing cure including accommodation and food in an Ayurveda resort will cost somewhere between £1000 and £1700. An Ayurveda clinic is slightly cheaper.

AYURVEDA RESORTS

Most hotels in Kerala offer Ayurvedic massages. Ayurveda centres are certified by a *Green Leaf* or *Olive Leaf*, both officially accredited by the government. Since 2012 even stricter standards have been applied. The directory can be found on the Kerala Tourism website, *www.keralatourism.org,* and it is also available through the India Tourist Office *(www.incredibleindia.com).*
Reputable Ayurvedic resorts include: the cgh earth hotel *Kalari Kovilakom (tel. 04923 263737 | www.kalarikovilakom. com)* housed in a former maharaja's palace*; the Thapovan Ayurvedic Centre* in

This ancient art of healing still works its magic – for both minor complaints and chronic conditions

Kovalam *(tel. 0471 2 48 04 53 | www. thapovan.com)*, the *Somatheeram Ayurvedic Health Resort*, Kovalam, *(tel. 0471 2 26 81 01 | www.somatheeram.org)*, which has received numerous awards (not to be confused with the Somatheeram Aryuvea Beach Resort); the *Poovar Island Resort (tel. 0471 2 57 36 49 | www. poovarislandresort.com),* which occupies its own small island; and the *Taj Ayurvedic Centre/The Gateway Hotel Calicut (tel. 0495 6 61 30 00),* which also has its own beach. Ayurveda has also been practised at the secluded INSIDER TIP *Kalappura Farmhouse* for 300 years *(bookings through www.keralatravelagent.com/ homestays-in-kerala/kalappura-farm house.html).*

AYURVEDA CLINICS

In Ayurveda resorts, the emphasis is mostly on treatments for internal body cleansing. In cases of chronic conditions such as rheumatism, diabetes, allergies, and cardiovascular or neurologically or metabolically related ailments, the best option is to go to a specialist Ayurvedic clinic such as the *Vaidya Ratnam Ayurveda Hospital* in Ollur/Thrissur *(www. vaidyaratnamcollege.org/hospital.php)* or *Ayurvaid (ayurvaid.com)*, India's first Ayurveda clinic to be certified according to international NABH clinical standards, which operates in Bangalore, Kochi and Chennai.

KERALA

The **600-km (375-mi) long Malabar Coast of southwest India corresponds exactly to the clichéd image of tropical beaches: warm as a bath, the Arabian Sea lapping against the endless stretches of palm-lined golden sand, beaches like Varkala with its red rocks, Alappuzha or the 9-km (5.5-mi) long Kovalam Beach.**

In the state of Kerala, which covers an area of 15,005 sq. mi., you will find within a short distance the most diverse landscapes and climatic zones right next to each other: coconut palm forests (Kerala is named after the palm tree, *kera*), rice paddies, more than 40 rivers, hill stations in cool highlands with their tea, coffee, spice and rubber plantations, mountain tribes still living by the same rituals and according to the same rhythm they have always done, powerful waterfalls thundering into the valleys and networks of trails stretching across hills and mountains. In between there are colonial cities and the enchanted world of the Backwaters, rainforests and jungle-like game reserves. A total of twelve nature reserves and two national parks provide protection for rare flora and fauna including the *Neelakurunji*, the blue flower, which blossoms only once every twelve years. Around 60 tigers live in the Periyar Tiger Sanctuary, while the Eravikulam National Park is home to the exotic Atlas moth and half the population of Nilgiri tahr – an endemic species of brown goat. Some of

Photo: In the Backwaters near Kollam

In the land where the peppercorn grows you're very close to paradise: India's loveliest holiday region is every traveller's dream

the world's rarest bird species can be found in the Thattekkady Bird Sanctuary ; the Silent Valley National Park has a relatively undisturbed evolutionary history stretching back at least 50 million years. And the Parambikulam Wildlife Sanctuary is one of the best places in the country to spot Indian bison, elephants and tigers. 'God's own country', as ex-Beatle Sir Paul McCartney calls Kerala, is fringed by glorious beaches, with everything from extensive luxury resorts to intimate boutique hotels to ecologically planned Ayurveda centres.

Indeed, ⭐ *Ayurveda (see p. 44)*, the ancient Indian art of healing, runs like a thread through Kerala. No wonder, for this was where it all started thousands of years ago. Kerala sees itself as one big temple of wellness. All kinds of massages are offered at every corner, on every beach, in every small hotel, sometimes very professional, sometimes less so, but always extremely relaxing.

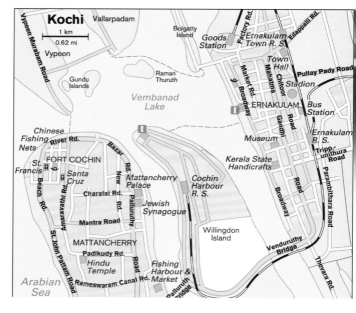

The land where the peppercorn grows is bordered by the Arabian Sea in the west and the Western Ghats, which in the hinterland rise to 2700m (8850ft). In 1502, the Portuguese mariner Vasco da Gama came ashore along this fertile coast on his third visit to India, with 15 ships and 800 men. But the booming trade in spices began over 2000 years ago and in the course of time it attracted Phoenicians, Greeks, Romans, Jews, Arabs, Chinese, Portuguese, Dutch and British. They all came back with an abundance of pepper, cardamom, sandalwood, cinnamon, ginger, saffron, tea, coffee and rubber.

In 1956, the rulers of the kingdoms of Malabar, Travancore and Cochin joined together to form the state of Kerala. Today, many different ethnic groups and religions live in peace with one another.

Christianity got a foothold in Kerala earlier than elsewhere. In AD 52, 'Doubting Thomas', one of Jesus' Twelve Apostles, is said to have landed on the Malabar Coast.

Kerala's educational attainment is higher than all the other Indian states. More than 90 percent of the approx. 32 million population read and write in the local Malayalam language. This is thanks to the Maharani of Trivandrum, who in 1817 decided that the state would take over the entire cost of educating its citizens. In every town and village there is an elementary school within a radius of 3km (2mi). In the state of Kerala the government is alternately run by the CPI or the CPI (M), Communist Party of India (Marxist), and the Congress Party: in many places you'll see the Red Flag with hammer and sickle flying.

In recent years Kerala has been at the forefront of Indian efforts to solve ubiquitous environmental problems. Ecotourism is the buzzword, and the evidence that this has indeed been implemented in many hotel complexes is visible, tangible and palpable. The 600-km (375-mi) coastline, stretching along the entire length of Kerala, is blessed with peaceful and often completely unspoilt, secluded sandy beaches, which rank among the best in the world. Offset by old lighthouses, nostalgic piers, high cliffs, fishing villages and impressive forts, each beach has its own character and charm. Nature and culture are the main aspects of a trip to Kerala.

Kathakali, a sophisticated dance drama, casts every audience under its spell. Kerala also has a rich repertoire of classic martial arts, which can be traced back more than a thousand years. The festivals are much more than mere entertainment, being deeply rooted in the ancient traditions of Kerala.

KOCHI (COCHIN)

MAP ON PAGE 48
(146 A4) *(ν D11)* **Kerala' second-largest city (pop. 604,000) is considered the oldest European settlement in India.**

On account of its picturesque situation in a natural harbour on the Malabar Coast and with its various districts that are spread across several peninsulas and outlying islands, Kochi is also called the 'Queen of the Arabian Sea'. On the mainland lies the district of Ernakulam. Ferries and bridges connect the islands of Willingdon, Bolghatty and Gundy in the harbour, Fort Cochin (which has retained the colonial name), Mattancherry at the southern end of the peninsula and Vallapadan and Vypeen north of Fort Cochin. Portuguese, Dutch and English settlers built most of the buildings in Fort Cochin,

---

★ **Ayurveda**
Ancient knowledge: the fount of good health and long life originated in Kerala → p. 44, 47

★ **Chinese fishing nets**
These bizarre contraptions off the beach at Fort Cochin look like giant spiders→ p. 50

★ **Kathakali**
Drums beat the rhythm in this classical dance drama → p. 53

★ **Brunton Boatyard**
A great view of the harbour from the former boatyard → p. 54

★ **Backwaters**
A vast network of enchanted waterways → p. 55, 72

★ **Marari Beach**
Picture postcard beach with palm trees → p. 56

★ **Munnar**
Living like a sahib among lush green tea plantations → p. 57

★ **Periyar Wildlife Sanctuary**
In South India's best-known nature reserve you can spot wild tigers, elephants and monkeys→ p. 58

★ **Varkala**
Take tea here: money can't buy the sunset view from the cliff top → p. 68

★ **Kollam**
Fantastic location between lake and sea → p. 70

MARCO POLO HIGHLIGHTS

KOCHI (COCHIN)

🏙 WHERE TO START?
Fort Cochin: Take the peninsula with the most interesting district as your starting point. To get there, walk or take a motor-rickshaw (approx. Rs 25) from *Ernakulum Train Station* to *Ernakulum Jetty*. From there by ferry to the *Cochin Customs Jetty*. The best form of transport in Fort Cochin's narrow alleyways is the cycle-rickshaw. You can take one to get to many of the sights, from the Chinese fishing nets to the Spice Market in the Mattancherry quarter.

which is also the name given to the peninsula.

In the early morning, just off the beach at Fort Cochin, Kochi's particular brand of magic reveals itself to the visitor with the emergence of Chinese fishing nets being pulled out of the water with their abundant catch. Or in the evening, watching from a boat when the weird contraptions supporting the nets are etched as black silhouettes against the setting sun. But Kochi's appeal also lies in the narrow alleyways of the Old Town with their many warehouses still wafting out their intense fragrance of spices. Kochi's history as a trading centre lives on in its grand colonial style mansions, in its old churches and in its continued importance as a busy fishing port.

SIGHTSEEING

BOLGHATTY PALACE
Built by the Dutch on Bolghatty Island in 1744, the former *Dutch Palace* was taken over by the British as their residence in 1909. Today it houses the *Hotel Bolghatty Palace*, which retains lots of the old colonial charm. Taking tea on the colonnaded veranda is a memorable experience. *Bolghatty Island | www.ktdc.com*

CHINESE FISHING NETS ★
Next to the ferry pier the beach is dominated by the distinctive Chinese fishing nets that are lowered into the water from a long cantilever supported by a bamboo frame anchored to a jetty. When the nets (known as lift nets) are hopefully full to bursting, they are pulled up again. You can go along and buy ● freshly caught shrimps and have them cooked for you on the spot. If you arrive early in the morning the fishermen may actually invite you onto the jetties to watch the nets being raised. Merchants first introduced the Chinese fishing nets to Kerala in the 13th century. The nets make an impressive photo, particularly at sunset, and the view from ᗡᙓ Vasco da Gama Square is one of the best. *Brunton Boatyard Hotel* has its own boat so that guests can see the sunset and the nets from the water. *Fort Cochin*

DUTCH CEMETERY
This was laid out by the Dutch in 1724 and renovated in 2007. A visit to the cemetery is particularly worthwhile because of its special atmosphere with the 104 gravestones bearing the names of mainly Dutch, but also of British sailors, merchants and soldiers. Visits can be arranged with the nearby St Francis Church. *Right next to the beach at Fort Cochin*

INDO-PORTUGUESE MUSEUM
This museum is housed in the present-day Bishop's Residence, which was first built in 1506 for the Portuguese Governor. Its five sections are devoted to Kerala's Christian heritage and display a variety of artefacts including a beautifully carved teak altar dating from the 16th

century and a sparkling crystal cross which refracts the sun's rays. *Tue–Sun 10am–5pm | Rs 25, first Thursday in the month admission free | Bishop's House, Fort Cochin*

JEWISH QUARTER IN MATTANCHERRY

Narrow alleyways full of souvenir and antique shops: all the jewellery, furniture and masks may look very tempting, but watch out for those export restrictions. It still gets very busy in the INSIDER TIP Spice Warehouses, also known as the *Spice Market*. Loads are hoisted to the lofts from brightly painted trucks. In the backyards are the large storerooms where you can buy spices very cheaply. The fragrance of nutmeg, cardamom, vanilla, cinnamon, sandalwood, ginger, coffee and tea wafts through the streets.

The *Paradesi Synagogue* is directly adjacent to the Mattancherry Palace. Built in 1568 by Jews whose forefathers arrived in Kerala as long ago as 69 BC, it is the oldest synagogue in India. As the last remaining of the seven synagogues that once stood in Cochin, it is used by the remaining Jewish community of about 20 souls. The floor of the synagogue is laid with blue and white Dutch tiles, and coloured-glass chandeliers hang from the ceiling. *Sun–Thu 10am–5pm | Synagogue Rd, Mattancherry*

SANTA CRUZ CATHEDRAL

At the southwestern tip of Fort Cochin and on the site of Kochi's first church built in 1505, stands the Roman Catholic cathedral. Constructed in 1903, it was modelled on the Rococo style and was only declared a cathedral in 1984, by Pope John Paul II. *Tue–Sat 9am–5pm, Sun 10.30am–1pm, mass daily 6am, 7am and 6pm | Rampath Rd, Fort Cochin | www.santacruzcathedralbasilica.org*

KERALA FOLKLORE THEATRE & MUSEUM

Today Kerala's folk art and artistic heritage are preserved in a former warehouse. The different architecture from three regions is displayed here: Malabar, Cochin and Travancore. You can also see masks, dance costumes, musical instruments, dolls, sculptures and manuscripts inscribed on palm leaves. Certified antiques are sold in the museum shop. There are also theatre performances at random times (Rs 500). *Daily 9.30am–7pm | Rs 100 | Folklore Junction, Theavara, Kochi | tel. 0484 2 66 54 52*

Magnificent colonial mix: the Paradesi Synagogue

KOCHI (COCHIN)

Typical Kerala: red tile roofs around a courtyard characterise the Mattancherry Palace

MATTANCHERRY PALACE/
DUTCH PALACE
This palace was built by the Portuguese in Mattancherry on the Fort Cochin peninsula in 1557 as a gift to the ruler of the day, Raja Vira Keralavarma. It was restored by the Dutch in the mid-17th century and is hence also known as the Dutch Palace. The building is a typical example of traditional Keralan architecture: white exterior walls with red roof tiles and an interior courtyard. In the courtyard stands a small temple, but the best thing about this maharaja's palace is the collection of murals depicting scenes from the Hindu epic, the Ramayana. The maharaja's bedroom, with its own erotic murals, is not always open to the public. *Sat–Thu 10am–5pm | Rs 5 | Mattancherry*

ST FRANCIS CHURCH
Built by Franciscan monks, first of wood and in 1516 of stone, this is the oldest European church in India. The white facade with its curvy outline is typical of many churches in South India. Inside the building you will find the slab marking the original grave of Vasco da Gama, who died in Cochin around Christmas 1524. His remains were later removed to Portugal. Other grave slabs bear the names of Portuguese and Dutch mariners. If the custodian is around, you might also get to see the old church books. *Mon–Sat 6am–7pm | Church Rd, Fort Cochin*

FOOD & DRINK

CAFÉ JEW TOWN
In the open *Ethnic Passage*, Annelies Damschen serves cappuccino, fresh juic-

es, chocolate and cheesecake as well as other European specialities. *The Ethnic Passage, Mattancherry, Fort Cochin | tel. 0484 2 22 56 01 | Budget*

INSIDER TIP ► CAFÉ PORT VIEW

With its views over the red rooftops of the Old Town and a pleasant cooling breeze, the roof terrace of the New Castle Gallery is an ideal place for a break. There's an old telescope on hand to enhance the amazing views that extend as far as Willingdon Island. The café serves Indian snacks, sandwiches and curries. *Bazar Rd, Mattancherry | tel. 0484 2 21 07 27 | Budget*

KASHI

This is an interesting mixture of art gallery and restaurant. You can get Italian cappuccino and *chai masala* – Indian spiced tea. There's also a small selection of European dishes on the breakfast and lunch menus. *Burgher Street, Fort Cochin | tel. 0484 2 21 57 69 | www.kashiartgallery.com | Budget–Moderate*

SEAGULL

Here you'll find good quality at very reasonable prices. Relax on the terrace while looking out over the harbour. Buffet at lunchtime. *2–18 Calvathy Rd, Fort Cochin | tel. 0484 2 21 71 72 | Budget*

SHOPPING

In Ernakulam, *Mahatma Gandhi Road*, otherwise known as MG Road, and *Broadway* are the main shopping thoroughfares. From Oriental and Western clothing to jewellery, cheap bags and suitcases, you can find (almost) everything here.

KATHAKALI

★ ● *Kathakali* is dance drama and the best-known dance form in South India. Silently, but with strong facial expressions and gestures, dancers enact scenes from the Hindu epics Ramayana and Mahabharata. The various characters are distinguished by the different colours of make-up on their faces. The long make-up process is seen as part of the whole performance, and spectators are very welcome to watch. The oldest and best Kathakali demonstration is offered by the *See India Foundation*. The make-up ceremony can be seen at 6pm and the daily performances begin at 6.45pm. *Admission Rs 130 | Kalathi Parambil Lane 7, Ernakulam | tel. 0484 2 37 64 71.*
The *Kerala Kathakali* Centre also stages the dance drama with an explanation of the gestures and colours before the show begins, daily 6.30pm (make-up procedure at 5pm). They also have daily performances of classical Indian music, and other Kerala dances on Saturdays (8.45pm). *Admission Rs 300 | K. B. Jacob Rd, Fort Cochin | tel. 0484 2 21 75 52 | www.kathakalicentre.com*
In *Greenix Village*, as well as traditional dances and martial arts they also demonstrate *Mohiniyattam* – a soft, flowing dance style with round movements, modelled on those of temple dancers. Make-up starts at 5pm, the dances at 6pm. *Admission Rs 225 | Kalvathy Rd, Fort Cochin | tel. 0484 2 21 71 00 | www.greenix.in*

KOCHI (COCHIN)

THE ETHNIC PASSAGE
This trendy arcade lies at the heart of the Mattancherry's Jewish quarter and houses bookstores, art galleries, leather shops and antique stores. *Mattancherry, Fort Cochin*

FABINDIA
Traditional patterns and materials produced in chic designs; there are five branches in Kochi alone: *26, Bay Pride Mall, Marine Drive; 1/279 Napier Street, Ft Cochin; Nucleus Mall, Maradu; Oberon Mall, NH Byepass – Edapally; Old Thevara Rd, Thamarapally, 39/4749 | www.fabindia.com*

THE KERALA STATE HANDICRAFTS DEVELOPMENT CORPORATION SHOWROOM – KAIRALI
Long name, big choice and fixed prices in this state-run emporium for handicrafts, materials, jewellery and much more. *MG Rd (at Jose Junction), Ernakulam*

MADONNA EXPORTS
Monasteries from all over India provide this non-profit centre with fine handicrafts at reasonable prices, including bobbin lace, batiste towels lovingly embroidered with elephants and flowers, napkins, children's clothes, and much more. *Synagogue Lane, VI/182, Jewish Quarter | Mattancherry*

INSIDER TIP NEW CASTLE GALLERY
Three floors packed full of art, jewellery, carpets, perfume, pashmina shawls. Bargaining essential. *Bazaar Rd, Mattancherry*

ENTERTAINMENT

AVA LOUNGE
Kochi's chic nightspot is in the *Dream Cochin* boutique hotel. Named after the film star Ava Gardner, the style is completely femme fatale: burnished golden sofas, gorgeous cushions, pure glamour. The mix of disco and nightclub attracts mainly Kochi's young smart set – not least on account of the steep (for India) admission price. *Fri/Sat 8.30pm-12.30am | admission Rs 2000, Wed usually ladies night (free admission for women) | S. A. Rd, Kadavanthara | www.dreamcochin.com*

EVENING BOAT TRIP
A romantic boat tour at sunset, once the temperatures have cooled – just delightful! With views of the harbour, Marine Drive, Bolgatty Island, Willingdon Island and the fishing nets. The tours depart from the harbour. *5.30–7pm | booking through the Tourism Reception Centre KTDC | tel. 0484 2 35 32 34 | www.ktdc.com*

WHERE TO STAY

BRUNTON BOATYARD ★
This hotel occupies a beautifully restored Victorian shipyard right on the harbour. The 22-room luxury establishment has an outdoor pool overlooking the water and the open arcades surrounding the shady inner courtyard are furnished with antiques. *River Rd, Fort Cochin | tel. 0484 2 215461 | wwrw.cghearth.com | Expensive*

CHITTOOR KOTTARAM
Something completely different: live like a king! Only closed groups of max. six people can stay at the 200-year-old residence of Keralan King Raja Verma, located on a backwater channel (1 large and 2 small bedrooms). Guests enjoy exclusive privacy, but convention dictates that they go barefoot inside. Service is top notch: the cooks prepare Keralan vegetarian specialities. *Chittoor Temple, op-*

*posite the SDOA School, Kottaram Rd,
Vaduthala | tel. 0484 3 011711 | www.cg-
hearth.com/chittoor-kottaram | Expensive*

NAPIER HOUSE

This old Dutch house with roof terrace
and large veranda has only eight rooms.
Very intimate atmosphere. *1/275 Napier
Lane, Fort Cochin | tel. 0484 2 215715 |
www.napierhouse.com | Moderate*

WHERE TO GO

ALAPPUZHA (ALLEPPEY)
(146 A4) (* flush D12*)

This 'Venice of the East' lies right on the
Arabian Sea and fully lives up to the epi-
thet bestowed on it by Viceroy Lord Cur-
zon. The city (pop. 177,000) was laid out
around two canals in 1776. Alappuzha,
with its endless palm groves, is also a

Backwaters supermarket: where merchants offer their wares from the water

SPENCER HOME

The eleven rooms in this old Portuguese
house are large and well maintained,
and each one enjoys a view of the lovely
garden. *1/298 Parade Rd, Fort Cochin | tel.
0484 2 215049 | spencerhome-fortkochi.
blogspot.com | Budget*

INFORMATION

TOURIST INFORMATION CENTRE
*At the pier | Ernakulum | tel. 0484
2 351015; at the bus station | Fort Cochin |
tel. 0484 2 216567*

starting point for excursions along the
★ *Backwaters (see p. 72),* Kerala's tight-
ly woven network of canals, lakes, lagoons and 44 rivers that is unique in the
world. Many migratory birds spend the
winter in this mostly untouched paradise.
In fact, most of the Backwater tours begin in Alappuzha. Some 900km (560mi)
of the 1900km (1180mi) of waterways
are navigable. Alappuzha is linked by
waterway to Kollam in the south and to
Kottayam in the east. There are regular
ferry connections between the three cities. Especially picturesque is the palm-

KOCHI (COCHIN)

lined *Alappuzha Beach,* complete with its lighthouse and pier. The lighthouse is more than 170 years old and has often featured in Bollywood movies.

Kottayam District is also home to the small town of *Kumarakom.* Here, the former teacher Raji Punnoose runs the *Bay Island Driftwood Museum (Tue–Sat 10am–5pm, Sun 11.30am–5pm | Chakranpadi | www.bayislandmuseum.com).* There is nothing else like it in India: for 25 years she has gathered driftwood from the Andaman and Nicobar Islands and has created from it a quite extraordinary artistic collection. The best hotel in the area, the *Vivanta by Taj Kumarakom (33 rooms | Kumarakom, Kottayam | tel. 0481 2 52 57 11 | www.vivantabytaj.com | Moderate–Expensive),* lies on Vembanad Lake, a Backwater lagoon. The main building is the 125-year-old *Baker's Bungalow.* Small villas built in Keralan style are ranged around the large pool and are partly furnished with antiques. The **INSIDER TIP** Coconut Palms Resort *(Thottapally, Kumarakodi, Pallana, Alleppey | tel. 0477 2 29 80 57, reservation tel. 0471 2 33 11 65 | Budget)* has its own houseboat and a lot of charm. It is a 200-year-old Keralan-style house with columned veranda, sweeping roof and eight charming rooms, just 400m from the Backwaters and 100m from the almost deserted *Pallana Beach.* Ayurveda, canoes and bicycles are also available. The **INSIDER TIP** Harbour Beer & Wine Bar *(Beach Rd | tel. 0477 2 23 07 67 | www.raheemresidency.com | Expensive)* next to the *Raheem Residency* boutique hotel, is a popular place to congregate, especially to watch the sun set over the ocean. For food there is *Kream Korner (Mullakal Rd | Budget),* which serves both vegetarian and non-vegetarian dishes, including a varied selection of *thalis.* Souvenir idea: some shops along the *Mullackal*

Shopping Street sell brightly-painted umbrellas. *50km (31mi) south*

CHERAI BEACH ☼ (146 A4) *(ⅅ D11)*
Kill two birds with one stone: sunrise over the Backwaters, then sunset over the sea. Both are possible from the same place, the glorious beach at the northern end of Vypeen Island, lined by dense palm groves and green rice fields. *By ferry (30 min) from Ernakulum*

ELEPHANT CAMP (146 B4) *(ⅅ D11)*
Situated 45km (28mi) northeast of Kochi is the village of Kodanad, at the edge of the Periyar National Park. At the time of the maharajas it was considered the largest elephant camp in South India. Since the introduction of a ban on elephant capture in 1974, Kodanad has just been a training centre for elephants. It's fun to watch the baby elephants as they bathe in the Periyar river morning and evening. A ride costs Rs 200. *Malayattur Forest Division | Kodanad | tel. 0484 2 64 90 52*

HILL PALACE MUSEUM TRIPUNITHURA (146 A4) *(ⅅ D11)*
This former residence of the king of Cochin has been converted into the largest ethno-archaeological museum in Kerala. The palace, built on a hill in 1865, comprises 49 separate buildings. Exhibits are arranged in 18 galleries and include amongst other items the royal throne, the crown, portraits of the ruler, 14th-century carvings, jewellery, porcelain and old musical instruments. *Tue–Sun 9am–12.30pm and 2–4.30pm | Rs 20. 10km (6mi) southeast*

MARARI BEACH ★ (146 A5) *(ⅅ D12)*
Located 70km (43mi) south of Kochi is the most beautiful beach in Kerala – Marari Beach on the so-called 'Spice Coast'. Still largely undiscovered by mass tour-

ism, this glorious idyll, with its fine sand, palm groves, small fishing villages and palm huts, is the perfect place to unwind. The *Hotel Marari Beach (Mararikulam, Alappuzha | tel. 0478 2 86 38 01 | www. cghearth.com | Moderate)*, has 52 Kerala-style bungalows and blends harmoniously with the landscape, hammocks swaying between some of the 3000-odd palm trees in the ground. It also grows its own organic fruit and vegetables.

MUNNAR ★ (146 B4) (∅ E11)

On account of their highland vegetation, the *Kanan Devan Hills* are often referred to as the Scotland of India. Nestled in the Western Ghats at a height of 1600m (5250ft), between the Mudrapuzha, Nallathanni and Kundala rivers, lies the pretty mountain town of Munnar (pop. 40,000). In colonial times the British came here for the cooler climes. Rising nearby is the highest mountain in South India, the 2695-m (8842-ft) Anamudi, but climbing to the summit is not al-

lowed because of the delicate vegetation. For mile after mile, rolling tea plantations stretch across the hillside, and 50 tons of tea are harvested in Munnar and its surrounding villages every single day. The *Tea Museum (daily 10am–4.30pm | Rs 100)* explains how the tea is processed and shows a film about its history; you can also buy tea straight from the producers, at very reasonable prices. Visiting a tea plantation can be arranged through the *Tourist Office (Main Rd | tel. 04865 23 15 16)*. The public paths snaking through the hilly plantations are perfect for hiking. It's also well worth visiting the *Atukkad Falls,* 8km (5mi) from Munnar, in the gorge at Pallivasal. A relative trickle for most of the year, during the monsoon in July and August it becomes a roaring cascade and home to sizeable colonies of birds. The route also leads past the ☀ *Pothamedu* viewpoint (6km/4mi from Munnar), which offers glorious views over the green waves of geometrically arranged tea gardens. About 7km

Lots of effort for one small cup: tea is still harvested by hand

KOCHI (COCHIN)

(4 mi) from Munnar is *Devikulam,* an idyllic mountain village. The INSIDER TIP flower meadow on the shores of Sita Devi Lake is a wonderful picnic spot. A further hiking destination lies 10km (6mi) away: *Yaymakad,* a beautiful area full of waterfalls, which plunge as much as 160m (500ft) into the depths.

It is to a coffee rather than a tea plantation that the hotel ✹ *Windermere Estate (Poathamedu, Munnar | www.windermereemunnar.com | tel. 0486 23 05 12 | Moderate–Expensive)* belongs. Here you will have a 360° panorama of the summits of the Western Ghats. A variety of exclusive garden villas with a total of 21 very tastefully furnished rooms blend harmoniously into the spectacular landscape. Accommodation of an unusual kind is provided at the INSIDER TIP Munnar Rock Resort *(2nd Mile, Pallivasal, Munnar | tel. 04865 216076 | www.munnarrock.com | Moderate),* which is perched, like a tree house, on top of an enormous cliff. There are only two rooms at the summit, a further six at the foot of the cliff. *130km (81mi) east*

PERIYAR WILDLIFE SANCTUARY ★
(146 B4) (*ψ E12*)

At an elevation of between 900–1800m (2950–5900ft) and easily reached by bus is the Periyar Wildlife Sanctuary *(daily 7am–5pm | admission Rs 300),* which stretches across an area of 300 sq. mi.. It was declared a tiger reserve in 1978. If you take a boat excursion on Periyar Lake, something that can be organised in Thekkady, you'll be able to spot entire herds of bathing elephants. Bookings can be made through the *Tiger Reserve Organisation (Ambady Junction, Lake Rd, Thekkady | tel. 04869 22 45 71)* or through the *Forest Information and Reservation Centre (tel. 04869 68 55 36)* in the same building. There are many dif-

ferent activities available, such as hiking for Rs 400, *Periyar Tiger Trail* (trekking and camping) for Rs 4000, *Bamboo Rafting* for Rs 1300 per person. Further information: *Tourism Information Thekkady | Junction in Kumily | tel. 0486 2 33 60 | www.periyartigerreserve.org.*

If possible, try to stay the night in Thekkady. The 55 thatched cabins of the ☺ INSIDER TIP Spice Village *(tel. 04869 22 45 14 | www.cghearth.com/spice-village | Moderate–Expensive)* are laid out like a tribal mountain village, in lush grounds covering an area of about 15 acres. In a live show *(daily 7.30–9.30pm),* a ranger tells you all about the wild animals that lurk around the perimeter; at cooking classes you can learn the secrets of the local cuisine and how to use and combine spices. This establishment puts the experience not luxury at the forefront, so everything from trekking to boat tours in the Periyar National Park as well as visits to spice and peppercorn farms is on offer *(see p. 117).* In addition they have a pool and offer Ayurveda. Because of their exemplary use of natural resources (their own paper recycling, organic vegetables, no TV, no air conditioning) the lodge has received numerous awards since it opened.

The Wildernest (Thekkady Rd | tel. 04869 22 40 30 | www.wildernest-kerala.com | Budget–Moderate) is a good B & B option. It is designed using natural materials, has ten bright, attractive rooms, some with balcony, others a small garden. The hearty breakfast should set you up for the entire day. *185km (115mi) southeast*

THRISSUR (TRICHUR)
(146 A3) (*ψ D11*)

Due to its rich history and architectural treasures, 'the city of Lord Shiva' is regarded as the cultural capital of Kerala. For centuries Thrissur (pop. 849,000)

Elephants parading side by side during the Pooram Festival at the Vadakkunathan Temple

belonged to the royal house of Kochi. Many rulers and dynasties, as well as colonial powers like Holland and Britain, were involved in the political and cultural growth of the city and its region. Splendid temples and remarkable churches bear witness to these developments.

Beautifully situated on a hill, surrounded by four *gopuram* (temple towers), the *Vadakkunnathan Temple (daily 4am–10.30am and 5–8.30pm)* dates from the 12th century. The walls of the temple are adorned with exquisite murals, the wooden beams decorated with beautiful carvings. In April/May time, during the Pooram Festival, the temple is also the destination of the grand procession of ornately decorated elephants. However, non-Hindus are forbidden from entering the temple, though they can set foot in the yard and walk around the outer wall. The *Guruvayur Ksetram Temple*, 30km (18 mi) northwest of Thrissur, is one of the most famous in all Kerala. Alongside the temple you can also visit the *Guruvayur Devaswom Institute (Mon–Fri 8am–4pm)* to see how the art of wall painting is taught.

The towers of the Basilica of Our *Lady of Dolours,* also known as Puthan Palli ('new church'), soar over the city. From the 87-m (285-ft) high ☆ *Bible Tower (Tue–Fri 10am–1pm and 2–6pm, Sat–Sun 10am–1pm and 2–7.30pm | High Rd)* you can enjoy a stunning panoramic view. The shining white building claims to be the largest church in Asia and is famous for its Indogothic style. Its foundation stone was laid in 1929, but the basilica was only consecrated in 1940. The Cathedral of *Our Lady of Lourdes* is best known for its underground chapel. *50km (31mi) north*

KOZHIKODE (CALICUT)

(143 F6) *(ᗰ D10)* **It is claimed that Vasco da Gama first stepped ashore on**

KOZHIKODE (CALICUT)

Indian soil at Kappad Beach. At least that's what the memorial plaque that has been erected there says. The date was 20 May 1498.

Historians think, however, that he actually landed at nearby Panthalayini in Kollam. Even the Italian globetrotter Marco Polo praised the beauty of Calicut. Today the *Jewel of Malabar* (pop. 430,000) offers a mixture of old temples, mosques, churches, markets and shopping thor-

set up their picnics on Mananchira Square, and the 3-km (2-mi) long Beach Road, some 2 km (approx. 1 mi) outside the centre by the sea, comes alive with people strolling and inline skating.

SIGHTSEEING

MISHKAL MOSQUE

It was about 700 years ago that an Arab ship owner by the name of Nakhooda

A very welcoming place: the Mishkal Mosque has 47 doors

oughfares. At the heart of the city is *Mananchira Square,* once the gigantic courtyard of a palace. Now the square is a green oasis with an artificial stream and an open-air stage for music and theatre. There are still a few colonial buildings standing in the old centre of the city, but many of the beautiful original houses have been replaced by modern functional structures – the city is gradually losing its character.

Kozhikode has a lot going on in the evening in particular. It is then that families

Mishkal had this mosque built. Constructed on 24 carved columns, it has a total of 47 doors and is primarily made of wood. Because the minaret is missing and the entrance looks more like a *gopuram*, the mosque bears a strong resemblance to Kerala's temple architecture. *Kuttichari, 2km (approx. 1 mi) outside Kozhikode*

PAZHASSIRAJA MUSEUM

This bungalow that once belonged to the Kottayam royal family dates from 1812. On display inside are murals, antique bronzes, ancient coins and crockery, while the art gallery next door exhibits the collections of various members of the royal family. *Tue–Sun 9am–1pm and 2–4.30pm | Rs 10 | East Hill | Karaparambu*

ST MARY'S CSI CHURCH

Dating from 1842, the largest Basel Mission church of the Malabar region is also known as the *English Church*. The Evangelical Missionary Society of Basel was founded in Switzerland in 1815, and one of its most important areas of operations was South India. St Mary's CSI Church has the only pipe organ in Kerala, a gift from St Ayden's Church in Cheltenham, England. *Daily 10am–1pm | Kannur Rd*

FOOD & DRINK

DAKSHIN

This very reasonably priced, purely vegetarian establishment is the best place to go for *dosas,* pizza and simple rice dishes. *17/43 Mavoor Rd | tel. 0495 2 72 26 48 | Budget*

KINGSBAY

This bright, friendly restaurant specialises in fish and seafood. Young people and travellers in particular appreciate the relaxed atmosphere and the view through the large window. *1414 Customs Rd | tel. 0496 4 05 44 22 | Moderate*

THE PARAGON RESTAURANT

Seafood features prominently at this upscale restaurant in the heart of the city. The art of authentic Malabar cuisine has been celebrated here ever since 1939 with dishes such as *Malabar Biryani* and *Coconut Chili Shrimps.* To go with them they mix their own original mocktails. *Kannur Rd | tel. 0495 6 70 20 | www.para gonrestaurant.net | Moderate*

SHOPPING

SM Street, actually *Sweet Meat Street,* is the main shopping thoroughfare in Kozhikode. Here they sell everything that the holidaymaker's heart desires – trendy clothes, modern jewellery and local handicrafts.

CAPITAL INTERNATIONAL BOOKS

You could browse in this bookshop for hours on end. The selection is diverse, and the prices for English-language books very low. You might even unearth a title here that you hadn't been able to find anywhere else. *Mon–Sat 8.30am–8pm, Sun 9am–6pm | 1 Street, Mavoor Rd*

MALABAR BAKERY

This is where you'll find the very best black *Calicut halwa,* a sweet that originally comes from Saudi Arabia and is considered a Kozhikode speciality. *Kallai Rd, Tali*

NUTAN HANDICRAFTS

A good place for souvenirs such as hand-embroidered fabrics of silk and cotton, statues of deities and beautiful woven napkins and tablecloths. *MM Ali Rd, Kairali*

BEACHES IN THE VICINITY

BEKAL (143 E5) (*ω C9*)

Deserted beaches, palm trees, Bekal Fort – the best preserved fortress in Kerala – and very peaceful, new resorts: Bekal is the new holiday region in the far north of Kerala on the Malabar Coast, 16km (10mi) south of Kasaragod and 192km (119mi) north of Calicut. Its potential was only recently discovered and is now gradually being realised. The Fort *(daily 9am–5pm | admission Rs 100)* was built in the 17th century and is located on a rocky promontory between two sandy beaches. An easily accessible ramp leads to the lookout tower. The ancient Anjenaya Temple with its idols in the stucco wall and an old mosque, said to have been built by Tipu Sultan, demonstrate the tolerance of different religions.

The smartest resort is the *LaLit (Bevoori Uduma Kasargod | tel. 04672 23 77 77 | www.thelalit.com | Expensive)* on the long beach to the north of the fort. Its Balinese-style buildings contain only 37 rooms spread across 26 acres of lush green. Each one is a flexible space and has its own private outdoor jacuzzi. Romantic dinners can be arranged on the anchored *Kettuvalam houseboat* (8 rooms). There's almost too much service: a 'holiday host' is on hand for every room. The spa also offers a large range of treatments.

BEYPORE BEACH (143 F6) (*𝄐 D10*)

This glorious sandy beach lies some 10km (6mi) south of Kozhikode. It is famous for its boatyard, where traditional dhows have been built ever since around 1500; today they still cast off from the beach in all directions.

KAPPAD BEACH (143 F6) (*𝄐 D10*)

It is on this palm-lined beach that Vasco da Gama is believed to have landed with his three ships on 20 May 1498. A temple thought to be more than 800 years old stands on the rocks. It has now been restored and painted in yellow, gold and black. Inside the building there is a platform *(peeda)*, which is worshipped as the seat of Bhadrakali, an incarnation of Goddess Parvati. Because she carries so many weapons with her, there are several golden swords with scimitar blades hanging in the temple.

KOZHIKODE BEACH (143 F6) (*𝄐 D10*)

This beach is famous for its sunsets. For a few rupees you can eat at one of the many stalls selling specialities such as *kallumekaya* (mussels). The old lighthouse and two piers, both over 100 years old, lend the beach a special charm.

Some call it a paradise beach, others their place of work: fishermen at Vallikunnu Beach

PADINHAREKARA BEACH ⛱
(146 A3) (*∅ D11*)
At the end of Tipu Sultan Road in Ponnani, 50km (31mi) south of Kozhikode, this beach provides a good vantage point from which to view the estuary of the Bharathapuzha River as it flows into the Arabian Sea.

INSIDER TIP ▶ VALLIKUNNU BEACH
(143 F6) (*∅ D10*)
This paradise beach lies 27km (17mi) south of Kozhikode and is completely lined with palm trees. From here the *Kadalundi* Bird Sanctuary can be reached on foot.

ENTERTAINMENT

CVN KALARI SANGAM
This is where you can see Kerala's very own martial art. Adversaries skilfully dodge each other as they lunge with swords and sticks, in a combat that depends on alertness and agility, using various steps and swift movements. *Daily 5–7pm | Rs 200 per performance | Nadakkavu | tel. 0495 2 76 82 14 | www.cvnkalari.com*

WHERE TO STAY

ALAKAPURI GUEST HOUSE
Established in 1958, this hotel stands in a delightful garden with a lotus pond and an abundance of flowers and trees. Its 40 spacious rooms have comfortable, old-style furniture, and there is a good restaurant and bar. The hotel is definitely one of the best in its category. *Moulana Mohamed Ali Rd, near the station | tel. 0495 2 72 34 51 | Budget*

KADAVU RESORT ⛱
As an Ayurveda resort, this establishment has been awarded Kerala's Green Leaf certification. The typical Kerala-style building has been here ever since the 11th century and is situated in a beautiful tropical garden right on the Backwaters. There are 97 rooms, 6 suites and 17 cottages and from the balconies and terraces, as well as one of the two restaurants (the *open-air Makkani* by the pool), you can watch the shimmering green Chaliyar River. A doctor monitors the Ayurveda treatments, which are applied very seriously. In addition, the resort offers yoga, cooking classes and houseboat tours. *Calicut Bypass Rd, Azhinjilam | tel. 0483 2 83 00 23 | www.kadavuresorts.com | Expensive*

INSIDER TIP ▶ NEELESHWAR HERMITAGE ☺
This epitome of a tropical paradise lies rather hidden among the palm trees on a secluded beach, where hammocks swing between the trees, pheasants strut around, tortoises are reared and an infinity pool seems to drop straight into the ocean. With no fewer than 18 thatched cottages all furnished in natural materials, the *Priya Spa* offers wellness, Ayurveda and yoga, plus the chef gives cooking classes. *Ozhinhavalappu, Kasaragod | tel. 0467 2 28 75 10 | www.neeleshwarhermitage.com | Moderate–Expensive*

OYSTER OPERA RESORT
Named after its owner – an oyster farmer who still uses traditional methods – this unusual resort is beautifully located on a promontory. The seven simple bamboo cottages, stilt and tree houses have names like 'Mussel', 'Oyster' and 'Shrimp'. The resort's own houseboat cruises through the backwaters. If they managed to clear away the plastic bottles and bags lying around, this could almost be called an 'eco' resort. *Tel. 094 47 17 64 65 | www.oysteropera.in | Budget*

RENAISSANCE COCHIN KAPPAD BEACH RESORT
This charming complex is located in a palm grove on the beach, with a pool. All of the four cottages have four rooms, each one enjoying a view of the ocean. It's the perfect place for an Ayurvedic cure. *Kappad Kannur Rd | tel. 0496 2 68 87 77 | www.renaissancekappad beach.com | Moderate–Expensive*

INFORMATION

TOURIST INFORMATION DTPC
Very helpful. *Manachira | tel. 0495 2 72 00 12*

TOURIST OFFICE
Kozhikode Railway Station | tel. 0495 2 70 26 06

WHERE TO GO

KANNUR (143 E5) (*Ø C9*)
Here, the old fort and the Parassinikada-vu Temple are well worth a visit. In 1505 the first Portuguese viceroy, Dom Francesco de Almeida, had the *St Angelo Fort (daily 8am–6pm | admission free)* strategically built on a rocky outcrop. Even today, visitors can see the dungeons, the secret passages leading to the sea, an old chapel and some cannon. Situated 18km (11mi) to the northeast, the *Parassinika-davu Sri Muthappan Temple (daily 5–8am and 4–8pm)* stands on the banks of the Valapattnam River, a popular place of pilgrimage. Legend has it that a child worked a miracle here. The holy shrine is even open to visitors. Information: *Tourist Office | Thaluk Office Compound | tel. 0497 2 70 63 36. 90km (56mi) north*

INSIDER TIP MAHÉ (143 F6) (*Ø C10*)
Also known as Mayyazhi, this charming little town (pop. 45,000) is situated on the estuary of the Mahé River. Its distinctly French atmosphere dates back to the time when it was an important French trading enclave. The police here continue to wear red caps just like in France, streets have French names and many of the locals speak the language of the early merchants. Its lovely riverside promenade is lined by old lanterns. *St Theresa's Church* is one of the oldest churches in the Malabar region, built in 1736 by the Italian Father Dominic. *65km (40mi) north*

INSIDER TIP WAYANAD
(143 F5–6) (*Ø D10*)
In the Nilgiri Hills, 105km (65mi) northeast of Kozhikode, the region of Wayanad, including the national park of the same name (133 sq. mi.) *(admission Rs 100),* is only just being discovered. But the tourist invasion hasn't arrived yet. Only a few nature lovers come here, to see the caves, go trekking in the jungle and marvel at the variety of exotic wildlife. Or get to know the *Adivasi* – the indigenous hill folk – and join them in celebrating the monsoon at the ● *Monsoon Splash festival* in Kalpetta – complete with mud football, crab racing, ox-cart or raft rides. Further information: *Wayanad Tourism Organisation | tel. 04936 25 53 08 | www.wayanadtourism.org*

THIRUVANAN-THAPURAM (TRIVANDRUM)

MAP INSIDE BACK COVER
(146 B6) (*Ø E13*) Magnificent colonial buildings characterise Kerala's capital city of Thiruvananthapuram with its 785,000 inhabitants.

WHERE TO START?
East Fort/Museum Square:
you can reach East Fort with buses
581 and 609 (orange), and nos. 5
and 8 will take you to Museum
Square. Linking these two points is
Mahatma Ghandi Road. From East
Fort to the west of the station it's a
short walk to the Sri Padmanabha
Swamy Temple and to the Chalai
Bazaar. On Museum Square you'll
find, for example, the Napier and
Kerala Museums, as well as various
galleries. The zoo is also nearby.

Just like Rome, the 'City of Sacred Snakes''
was built on seven hills. Red roof tiles,
modern shops and small cafés reinforce
the European impression. In addition,
the former Trivandrum is important as
the setting-off point for Kerala's most
popular beach, Kovalam. It lies just 16km
(10mi) to the south and can easily be
reached by bus or motor-rickshaw.

SIGHTSEEING

KUTHIRAMALIKA PALACE

This enormous two-storey palace with
more than 80 rooms is also known as the
Puthen Mailika. It was built in 1844 for
Maharaja Swathi Thirunal, in typical
Keralan style, with magnificent carvings
and life-size figures. Some parts of the
building have been turned into a museum. Outstanding carved exhibits include
the 140-year-old ivory throne and wood-
en horses in the upper gallery, as well as
palanquins, weapons and life-size
Kathakali mannequins. *Tue–Sun 8.30am–
12.30pm and 3–4.45pm | Rs 35 | East Fort*

NAPIER MUSEUM

Also known as the *Thiruvananthapuram
Museum*. Designed in 19th-century red-
and-white Indo-Sarenic style, the build-

A real challenge for all the senses: the daily bustle of Trivandrum's streets

ing is impressive enough on its own. But it also houses a large collection of South Indian art, including statues of bronze and wood from the 11th–18th century, jewellery from the 10th–14th century, a temple chariot made of rosewood with carved mythological figures from 1847 and a replica of a typical Keralan house. *Daily 10am–5pm | Rs 25 | Public Park*

INSIDER TIP PAZHAVANGADI GANAPATHY TEMPLE

Every morning, at varying times according to the season, hundreds of Hindus congregate in the courtyard of this black stone temple to smash between 20,000 and 30,000 coconuts as an offering to the elephant-headed god Ganesh. A loud murmur like a swarm of bees echoes around the courtyard for while breaking the coconuts the faithful offer a prayer. The local statue of *Lord Ganapathy* (Ganesh) is so strongly revered here because, unusually, the right leg of the god is bent as if in the lotus posture. *East Fort*

SRI CHITRA ART GALLERY

This is situated opposite the Napier Museum and amongst other items displays pictures by the painter Raja Rai Varma (1848–1906), known for his detailed depictions of scenes from the religious epics Mahabharata and Ramayana. In addition, there are exquisite works by Rajputs and Moghuls, who at various times had a huge influence on the cultural development of India. *Tue–Sun 10am–4.45pm, Wed afternoons only | Rs 30 | Public Park*

SRI PADMANABHA SWAMY TEMPLE

In June 2011 this temple suddenly achieved overnight fame, because in two of its six underground chambers, which had been closed for 130 years, a hoard of treasure worth approx. 7–9 billion £ was discovered, amassed from the donations of former benefactors in the form of diamonds, rubies, emeralds, gold and silver. Dating from the 17th century, the temple is dedicated to the god Vishnu. Its 17-m (56-ft) high entrance tower is visible from afar. Non-Hindus can only admire the holy temple from the outside, but twice a year everyone has a chance to glimpse the gilded statue of Sri Padmanabha, an incarnation of Vishnu: in March/April and in October/November, when it is carried to the sea for a ritual bath. *At the southern end of the MG Rd*

ZOO

The large park was opened by the Maharaja of Travancore in 1859 as one of the first zoological gardens in India. Laid out like a botanic garden, with its many trees, lakes and lawns it is considered the most natural zoo in the country. It is home to a total of 75 animal species, including such rare specimens as the Bengal tiger and the Asian lion. *Tue–Sun 9am–6.15pm | Rs 10, camera Rs 10, video camera Rs 100 | PMG Junction*

FOOD & DRINK

INSIDER TIP ARYA NIVAS

The best vegetarian restaurant in the city for South Indian specialities, and also for Punjabi dishes, *tandoori* and delicious *dosas*. *In Hotel Arya Nivas, right at the station | tel. 0484 2 38 10 38 | Budget*

KALAVARA

Amidst the bustle of Trivandrum this three-storey restaurant is like an oasis of calm. In addition to Indian and European dishes, the restaurant also specialises in Chinese cuisine. The best place to sit is under the sun umbrellas on the roof terrace. *Press Rd | tel. 0471 2 33 13 62 | Moderate*

SHOPPING

On the main shopping thoroughfare *MG Road* you'll also find *Chalai Bazaar* and *Connemara Market,* where you can buy freshly caught fish (mornings only), fruit, vegetables and spices, as well as beauti-

BEACHES IN THE VICINITY

KOVALAM BEACH (146 B6) *(𝄽 E13)*
This is considered Kerala's most important beach, and lies 16km (10mi) south of Trivandrum. Kovalam consists of a small town and a series of three connecting

A different world south of Kerala's capital: Kovalam Beach consists of three bays

ful materials, gold jewellery and even bags and suitcases (bargaining essential).

KRISHNAN NAIR & SONS
As far as jewellery and watches are concerned, this is one place you can trust. This traditional jeweller has been established since 1911. *Padmavilasom Rd, Fort | www.krishnannairandsons.com*

S. M.S. M. HANDICRAFT EMPORIUM
One of the best arts and crafts, jewellery and material shops – with fixed prices. *Puthenchanthai*

bays, Lighthouse, Hawah and Samudra, all characterised by their unusual rock formations. The southernmost section, *Lighthouse Beach,* is named after the 35-m (115-ft) high lighthouse on Kurumkal Hill. Many stalls selling colourful travellers' clothing, fast food and massage deals line *Hawah Beach* in particular. However, Lighthouse and Hawah beaches are no longer as clean as they once were. The recently renovated seafront promenade is almost exclusively shops and hotels, but you are compensated by the sight of fishermen pulling their boats up on the beach in the evenings.

One recommended hotel is *The Leela Kovalam (tel. 0471 2 48 01 01 | www.the leela.com | Expensive)*. This extensive complex with a total of 186 rooms is built on terraces leading down to the sea. It has two infinity pools, seven restaurants and a large spa. The *Thapovan Resort (Nellikunnu, Mulloor | tel. 0471 2 48 04 53 | www.thapovan.com | Moderate)* with its 31 rooms housed in small bungalows, stretches across a sloping garden down to Nellikunnu beach. It has made a reputation for itself as an Ayurveda resort. The ☼ uppermost of its two restaurants offers a fantastic panoramic view of the sea. The owner will direct guests to local events, from the food festival in the neighbouring village to temple festivals; his excursions will

LOW BUDGET

▶ The cheapest and most exciting way to get to know Kerala and its inhabitants is through *homestays*, that is private accommodation. You can go on excursions, enjoy eating authentic food with local people and get their advice and tips. You can find addresses at local *tourist offices* or at *www.keralahomestays.com*.

▶ Far, far cheaper than a houseboat is discovering the Backwaters *(see p. 72)* by public ferry. They regularly ply between Alappuzha, Kollam and Kottayam. The 2½-hour journey between Alappuzha and Kottayam, for example, crosses Vembanad Lake, an important habitat for birds, and costs only Rs 12. The public ferries operate daily from 7.30am to 5.30pm.

not cost any more than the taxi journey. Meanwhile, the view from the ☼ INSIDER TIP terrace of the Rock Holm Hotel *(Lighthouse Rd, Vizhinja | tel. 0471 2 48 03 06 | www.rockholm.com | Budget)* is priceless, with the lighthouse and the palm-lined bay below. Local speciality: *fish molee*, a fish curry with coconut rice. No alcohol. The trendiest restaurant is the *Fusion (Lighthouse Beach | tel. 0471 2 48 01 79 | Budget–Moderate)*, which offers the choice of three cuisines: Eastern, Western and, naturally, Fusion – the combination of a variety of influences. There's always something going on in the evenings around the bars and restaurants on Kovalam's beach promenade. Good live music is played at the open-air *Beatles Restaurant (tel. 0471 2 48 31 56 | Moderate)*. If you fancy some cakes, try the ☼ *German Bakery (Lighthouse Beach | tel. 0471 2 48 01 79)* – especially for breakfast on the terrace. Although it's more like a restaurant than a bakery, you can get delicious cakes, waffles and pancakes there. The sea view is free.

VARKALA ★ ☼ (146 B5) (𝄞 E13)

At the base of the red cliffs, *Panasam Beach* extends for just under a kilometre. It is much less crowded than Kovalam Beach. However, there's a certain clash of cultures in Varkala: on the one hand, the girls in bikinis who don't take much notice of the ban on topless sunbathing; on the other, the ● practising Hindus, who, early in the morning, at the southern end of the beach and in the presence of white-robed priests, hold ceremonies for their departed loved-ones, five days after their death, and then cast the consecrated ashes into the sea. Afterwards, they take a spiritually healing bath in the pool of the *Janardhanaswamy Temple*. Sixty steps lead up to the 2000-year-old temple, but non-Hindus are not allowed to enter its sanctuary.

For holidaymakers, backpackers and dropouts alike, the place to head for in Varkala is the ● ☀ *Path on the Cliff*. Along this paved path there are hotels and guest houses one after another, col-

akhilbeachresort.com | Moderate) the eleven deluxe cottages and the six rooms in the main building are surrounded by a pleasant garden; they also offer Ayurveda, yoga and meditation.

Beneath the cliff, right on the south beach, lies the ☀ *Hindustan Beach Re-*

The much-visited Varkala is a good pitch for street traders and craftspeople

ourful clothes blowing in the wind in front of the many shops and boutiques, Ayurveda offered at every corner and, in front of the bars, cafés and restaurants, chairs facing the sea ready for the sunset. The cliff path is being continually extended, so that further resorts can be built. After all, it's up here where you will find the best views, such as from the *Kerala Bamboo House (Papanasam Cliff, Kurak-kani | tel. 098 95 27 09 93 | www.kerala bamboohouse.in | Budget)*, where 21 huts and an Ayurveda centre have been built entirely from materials found in the forest. Just one disadvantage: no hot water. At the *Akhil Beach Resort (Papanasam Cliff | tel. 098 95 27 09 93 | www.*

treat (Papanasam Beach | tel. 0470 2 60 42 54 | www.hindustanbeachretreat. com | Moderate), which also serves as accommodation for pilgrims. Here too, there are great views of the sea from the rooftop restaurant and all 27 rooms and three suites. There's also a pool, as well as Ayurveda treatments and yoga. A little way away from the beach, the *Eden Garden Ayurvedic Retreat (Papanasam Beach | tel. 0470 2 60 39 10 | www.eden garden.in | Budget–Moderate)* offers a wide range of treatments. The red houses with twelve rooms are situated under palm trees and by a fish pond. *50km (31mi) northwest*

ENTERTAINMENT

NEERA BAR ☼

The best thing about this bar is the incredible view of the sea. But they also mix good cocktails, have a wide selection of wines and serve sushi and tapas. There's only room for about 30 people, and the lounge atmosphere is enhanced by appropriate music and bar billiards. Smokers congregate on the adjacent terrace. *Daily 11am–11pm | Kovalam | Vivanta by Taj Hotel | G.V. Raja Vattappara Rd | tel. 0471 6 61 30 00*

WHERE TO STAY

NANDANAM PARK

This new hotel is nice and bright, with clean lines throughout. It has 32 rooms, two restaurants and an airy ☼ rooftop café, which has views over the city. A modern establishment, it lies in the heart of the city, a kilometre or so from the station. *Nandavanam Rd, opposite the A. R. Police Camp, Palayam | tel. 0471 2 33 66 11 | www.nandanampark.com | Budget*

RESIDENCY TOWER

This white building in the heart of the city is reminiscent of Miami. The 63 rooms are bright and modern, and there's a pool as well as a rooftop restaurant. *Press Rd | tel. 0471 2 33 16 61 | www.residencytower.com | Moderate*

THAMBURU INTERNATIONAL

Although this modern hotel lies right opposite Trivandrum station, it is in fact very quiet. It has 35 rooms, a good restaurant and a relaxing lobby. *Aristo Junction | tel. 0471 2 32 19 74 | www.thamburu.com | Moderate*

INFORMATION

TOURIST INFORMATION CENTRE

Park View, next to the museum | tel. 0471 2 32 11 32 | www.keralatourism.org

TOURIST FACILITATION CENTRE

In the Guest House Compound, next to the bus station, Kovalam | tel. 0471 2 48 00 85

WHERE TO GO

KOLLAM (QUILON) ★
(146 B5) (*(Ø) D12*)

Kollam has a population of 361,000 and lies between the sea and the 16-km (10-mi) long Ashtamudi Lake, the gateway to the Backwaters. The architecture is characterised by typical Keralan wooden houses with red-tile roofs. Kollam is also famous for the processing of cashew nuts, and large houseboats are built in the Alumkadavu boatyard. In many places in town, coconut fibres are made into mats and ropes. Situated nearby is the famous *Amritapuri Ashram (see p. 23)* of Mata Amritanandamayi *(tel. 0476 3 24 10 64 | www.amritapuri.org)*.

KONNI (146 B5) (*(Ø) E12*)

Around 68km (42mi) north of Thiruvananthapuram, near Pathanamthitta, lies the small settlement of Konni. For animal lovers it's worth making the trip on account of the *Elephant Training Centre (daily 10am–5.30pm | Rs 60)*. Established as long ago as 1941, it is the oldest in India. Pachyderms that have been abandoned by the herd or found wounded are accommodated in enormous wooden stables. Visitors can watch them bathing in the Achankovil River and also try their hand at riding. Recently, a butterfly museum has been installed at the camp. Just one kilometre away lies the elegant *Contour Jungle Resort (tel. 0468 2 24 97 49 | www.contourjungle.com | Expensive)*, which has 14 rooms in cottages.

NEYYAR WILDLIFE SANCTUARY
(146 B–C6) *(ΩΩ E13)*

With its varied terrain of rushing streams, slopes and meadows, this game park is ideal for a walk or a hike that could include an ascent of the 1868-m (6129-ft) high *Agashthyamala Peak* (three or four hours depending on fitness). Trekking permits are issued by the *Kerala Forestry & Wildlife Department (tel. 00261 22 71 43 | www.keralaforest.org)*, but only in January/February. In the jungle-like park, which covers 46 sq. mi. around the Neyyar dam lake, you can see elephants, muntjac and mountain goats. Admission Rs 100, *Jeep safaris Rs 250 per jeep plus Rs 10 for the guide | Information office at the entrance | tel. 0471 2 36 07 62 | 30 km (21mi) east*

PONMUDI **(146 B6)** *(ΩΩ E13)*

This idyllic hill station lies 61km (38mi) northeast of Trivandrum at a height of 915m (3002ft). It is the perfect place for extended, easy walks past bubbling springs and wild orchids. There are also numerous winding paths meandering through tea and rubber plantations. One of them leads to the *Meenmutti waterfall*, 15km (9mi) away, where the *Kallar River* plunges into the depths. Recommended accommodation is the *Ponmudi Tourist Resort (tel. 0472 2 89 02 30 | Budget)* with 24 rooms and ten cottages. It lies in a garden among wooded hills. The restaurant is purely vegetarian, but they do serve beer.

POOVAR ISLAND ☺ **(146 B6)** *(ΩΩ E13)*

This paradise island lies between the Backwaters and the open sea. Even though boats cross to the offshore sand-

bar, swimming in the sea is not allowed because of the strong current. In return, you have two resorts that offer maximum relaxation in complete seclusion, both specialising in Ayurveda. In addition, the *Poovar Island Resort (tel. 0471 2 57 36 49 | www.poovarislandresort. com | Moderate)* has its very own dentist so you can catch up on your dental care.

In a rubber plantation near Ponmudi

Spread across an area of 62 acres are villas housing 78 rooms, as well as 16 overwater bungalows. Also: two pools, beauty salon, no cars, no plastic, biogas, solar power. Green Leaf certification.

On the neighbouring property stands the *Estuary Island Resort (www.estuaryisland. com | Moderate)*, spread across 37 acres with 71 rooms in cottages and a three-storey main building. They also have a pool and Ayurveda centre. *12km (7mi) south*

BACKWATERS

Kerala's real highlights are the ⭐ *Backwaters*, a network of around 1900km (1200mi) of canals, which at certain points expand into large lakes. The district of *Alappuzha* (Alleppey) is regarded as the 'Venice of Kerala'. That's where the large ● houseboats are moored; modelled on the old rice boats, they are made of wood and tied together with coconut fibres. The main routes run between *Kollam* (Quilon) and Alappuzha, the principal centre of Backwater tours. To get a taste, you can take one of the public ferries *(see p. 68)*.

Just a relatively short trip on a motorboat will give you a good impression of the magical, watery world of the Backwaters, with its stunning flora and fauna. Sometimes, they widen into large lakes like Ashtamudi, Kayamkulam and Vembanad. And sometimes, such as at Trikunnipuzha, the canals get so narrow that you can reach out and touch the palm leaves on the bank.

The Backwaters run like arteries through villages, rice fields and palm groves. Canoes, loaded with vegetables, tapioca, areca and cashew nuts, regularly cross the path of the tour boats. Waving children will often run after the boats along the banks. Stretched between the palm trees, you'll also see ropes, on which the *toddy tapper* balances as he taps the freshly fermented coconut juice. The house- and motorboats usually stop at one of the small *toddy bars* so you can have a taste, together with a piece of grilled *karimeen,* the local Backwaters fish. Chanting emanates from Hindu temples and thousands of migrating birds perch in the trees.

HOUSEBOAT TOURS

Today's houseboats are converted *kettuvalloms,* cargo boats that once transported people and material, rice and spices to Kochi harbour. *Kettu* means to sew, *vallom* means boat; the boat builders use only wood and coconut twine, not a single nail. Navigating the narrow canals requires considerable skill, and long poles are often deployed. With several closed cabins, shower/WC, dining area and sun deck, the converted boats offer tourists lots of comfort. You can sail through the backwaters for several days; a cook will look after the catering. Recent years have seen a considerable increase in the number of houseboats on the

Life on the water: simply go with the flow along a labyrinth of delightful lakes and canals

Backwaters, and now there are over a thousand of them, run by more than 50 operators. For laymen, it is not easy to tell the differences in quality. Either book a tour from home through a specialist operator, go through a good agent in India, or the *Tourist Office* in Alappuzha or Kollam. To be on the really safe side you can also think about arranging a tour through a good hotel that has its own houseboat.

DAY TRIPS

It's also possible to do a day trip aboard a houseboat, costing anywhere between Rs 3000 and Rs 7000 per boat. You can book, for example, with a large operator such as 😊 *Rainbow Cruises (tel. 0477 2 26 13 75 | www.rainbowcruises.in)*, which, like some other companies, tries to increase environmental awareness among the villagers. For a ride on a motorboat, expect to pay approx. Rs 300 per person per hour.

Kollam–Alappuzha tours commence daily at 10.30am from the pier, trips to the villages aboard a *country boat* are offered daily between 9am–1pm and 2–6pm. Info: *DTPC Tourist Information Office | KSRTC Bus Stand, Kollam*
There are also daily tours running in the opposite direction, from Alappuzha to Kollam: the Backwater Cruise takes eight hours and costs Rs 300 per person *(10.30am from DTPC pier)*; from Alappuzha to Kumarakom it leaves from the DTPC pier daily at 11am *(Rs 150, minimum 10 people)*. Or you can hire a rowing boat to tour the villages *(Rs 150 per hr/person)*. Information: *The Administrative Office DTPC (by the pier, Alappuzha | tel. 0477 2 25 33 08 | www.dtpcalappuzha. com)* or *Tourist Reception Centre DTPC (by the KSRTC bus station, Alappuzha | tel. 0477 2 25 17 96)*.

KARNATAKA

Architectural jewels and historical sites wherever you roam. Magnificent palaces, richly decorated temples, mystical mosques. No Indian state has such a rich history or so many silent but also eloquent witnesses to long-lost cultures as Karnataka.

Rather than being confronted with boring, run-of-the-mill history, visible only in museums and ruins, visitors to Karnataka will experience a living past, mostly within our grasp, sometimes beyond belief. Gaze in amazement at elaborate stone reliefs depicting images of a time in which we also have our roots: reliefs festooned with figures of deities that appear to jump out of the stonework; temple dancers that seemingly gyrate to unheard melodies; erotic depictions that

are enough to make the prudish blush. Nowhere else in India has such fine, vivid stone carvings as those created here in Karnataka. All these images open windows onto a world full of fairy tales and mysticism – like one enormous reference work of Indian mythology. The epitome of the fairy-tale splendour of ancient princely glory is the Maharaja's Palace in Mysore, which looks almost unworldly when illuminated at night.

As far as tourists are concerned, Karnataka does not particularly feature as a seaside destination, although it does have its fair share of fine beaches, such as the famed Om Bay, as well as a dazzling underwater world just waiting to be discovered by divers. But it's in its scenic beauty that the 192,000-sq. km (73,000-

Photo: Bangalore Palace

Ancient sites and modern cities: travel through time back to India's mythical past – and into its promising future

sq. mi) state comes into its own, with a fascinating kaleidoscope of the natural world from bizarre rock formations to huge national parks full of exotic fauna and flora. Most of India's tigers survive in the game parks of Karnataka, as well as a quarter of the world's population of Asian elephants. Then there are the enchanted jungles and high mountains of the Western Ghats, which stretch for hundreds of miles through Karnataka and give trekkers and rock climbers a real treat. Spectacular waterfalls like the Jog Falls, which in the monsoon become mighty forces of nature. And lush green tea plantations that wrap themselves around gentle hills flecked with colonial hill stations.

Karnataka also offers the most exciting contrasts. In Bengaluru, formerly Bangalore, India's own Silicon Valley, the technological future of India has well and truly begun. The city has also made a name for itself as a centre for specialist medical treatments, which work out far cheaper here than in Europe. On the other hand, it can sometimes seem as though the wheel of time has almost come to a complete standstill, when somewhere, amid the barren, rocky landscape, an ancient ox cart emerges out of the haze.

BENGALURU (BANGALORE)

MAP INSIDE BACK COVER
(144 C4) *(🕮 E8–9)* **With its highways and office buildings, its parks and botanical garden, this garden city (pop. 8.5 million) at a height of 949m (3114ft) looks decidedly European. But even here the Indian past is noticeable, and**

Exotic flora has been collected in the Botanical Gardens since the 18th century

there are temples and museums worth visiting.
And with a temperature range of 14 to 33 degrees centigrade, it has a very pleas-

> **WHERE TO START?**
> **Cauvery Handicraft building:** Arts and crafts are sold here, at the junction of Brigade Road and MG Road. It is not far from the *Shivaji Nagar* bus stand or the nearby underground station. From here, it is easy to reach Cubbon Park and the Lalbagh Botanical Gardens on foot. Buses go to the Tipu Sultan Palace in Old Bangalore, to the Nandi Bull Temple, Bangalore Palace and the Government Museum.

ant climate. You can also clearly see the future that is envisaged for this IT metropolis, as it spreads out further and further, building sites all over the place. But the eternal traffic congestion calls for strong nerves.

SIGHTSEEING

BANGALORE PALACE
The royal palace was built in 1887 and, with its turrets and towers, strongly resembles Windsor Castle. Because the Maharaja still uses some of the rooms when he is in Bangalore, guided tours are by prior arrangement only. Concerts often take place in the grounds, with the likes of the Rolling Stones, Sting, Scorpions and Deep Purple having performed here over the years. *Closed Sun | Rs 200, photos Rs 500 | Palace Rd*

CUBBON PARK
Covering 320 acres, this lovely park, adorned with flowers, fountains and statues, is the green heart of the city. It is home to the state library, the *Government Museum* with its sculptures *(Rs 4)* and the *Venkatappa Art Gallery* where more than 600 paintings are on display

over three floors. That's not forgetting the *Technological and Industrial Museum (Rs 25)*. *All open Tue–Sun 10am–5pm | Queen's Street*

LALBAGH BOTANICAL GARDENS ★

Here, over an area of approx. 250 acres, you will find the largest collection of tropical and subtropical plants in India, alongside centuries-old trees. The garden was laid out in 1760. Flower shows marking India's National Holiday (26 January) and Independence Day (15 August) are organised in the glass house, which was modelled on Crystal Palace in London.; there are also folklore evenings every second Sunday. *Daily 6am–7pm | Rs 10, free admission 6–9am and 6–7pm | KH Rd | www.lalbaghgardens.com*

NANDI BULL IN THE BULL TEMPLE

The bull Nandi is the mount of the god Shiva and is worshipped accordingly. The Bull Monument in the *Bull Temple* of Bengaluru is of grey granite, almost 5m (16ft) high and 6m (20ft) long. The statue is polished daily and decorated with garlands. *Bull Temple Rd, Basavanagudi*

FOOD & DRINK

BLUE GINGER IN THE TAJ WEST END ●
Authentic Vietnamese dishes, prepared by Vietnamese cooks, are prepared under an open thatched roof in the middle of a tropical garden. Guests travelling alone are given a INSIDER TIP goldfish in a bowl on the table for company. Next door is *The Blue Bar,* one of the city's fashionable nightspots. *Taj West End | 25 Racecourse Rd | tel. 080 66 60 56 60 | www.tajhotels.com | Expensive*

MR BEANS – THE COFFEE LOUNGE

Those who can't do without their Italian coffee routine complete with latte macchiato, espresso, cappuccino and 30 different types of iced coffee have come to the right place in this smart white villa. The finest Indian tea is also served here, and in the stylish ambience the various fruit flavours of a shisha also taste good. *Koramangala, 3. Block | tel. 080 41115717 | www.mrbeans.in | Budget*

MTR (MAVALLI TIFFIN ROOMS)

Tiffin means snack, and that is the speciality of MTR, Bengaluru's oldest vegetarian restaurant. But breakfasts, lunch and evening meals are also served. You should definitely give the *idlis* a try – delicious little pancakes made of rice and semolina with a spicy sauce. Dark furniture helps to retain the atmosphere of the 1920s. *11 Lalbagh Rd, near the Botanical Gardens | tel. 080 22220022 | Budget*

ULLA'S REFRESHMENTS

From the 🏔 terrace on the first floor you can enjoy a great view over the bustle of MG Road. The vegetarian dishes here can be taken as snacks or as complete meals.

MG Rd, Public Utility Bldg | tel. 080 25587486 | Moderate

SHOPPING

COTTAGE CRAFTS EMPORIUM

Mainly jewellery, carpets and silk. The owner Babloo Jain will figure out your lucky birthstone and also tell your fortune. *122/2 Monarch Chambers, Infantry Rd*

INSIDER TIP ▶ GANGARAM BOOK STORE

Bookworms are sure to find what they're looking for amongst the thousands of titles spread across three floors. The friendly staff will look out a required volume on request. The shop, with its many reading corners, has been around for more than 30 years. *72 MG Rd*

VIMOR

One of the best shops in town for saris and material, including hand-woven cottons and silks. Ready-made clothing such as scarves or ladies Punjabi suits with

Universal pleasures: shopping and phoning in Bengaluru, just like in every city worldwide

narrow trousers and long tunics also available. *3164, S-Skoneria, crossing 1 and 2 Main, at Blind Love, ESI-Domlur Service Rd, Indiranagar | www.bandhej.com*

ENTERTAINMENT

Bengaluru has the large international business contingent to thank for its high density of pubs and bars. In the pubs, alcohol can only be served until 11.30pm

HARD ROCK CAFÉ

The huge cult café is divided up into three different areas – a restaurant with seating for 100, a bar and an open courtyard, as well as a Rock Shop. Like Hard Rock Cafés all over the world, this one is decorated with memorabilia and collectibles from rock greats. With a bit of luck you might see a jam session going on. *Mon–Sun noon–11.30pm | 40 St Marks Rd | tel. 080 41 24 22 22*

LOCK & LOAD PUB

This mixture of pub, disco and bar in the Chairman's Resort is one of Bangalore's Top Ten. Everything is done in Wild West style, from old comic-book images and waiters dressed in cowboy clothes to a huge dance floor with constantly changing, coloured light reflections and saddles as chairs. There's an in-house DJ to look after the sound. *Mon–Sat 11.30am–11pm | No. 14/1, Kodigehalli Main Rd, Sahakar Nagar, Hebbal, near the Twin Towers | www.chairmansresort.com*

SHIRO

After Mumbai and Goa, Shiro has now taken Bangalore by storm as the place for fine dining. There is opulence on all three levels of this restaurant/lounge complex: statues of Greek gods, fountains, Buddha statues and a DJ console set in the 'sky'. And right at the top is Bangalore's largest roof terrace. The menu offers a range of Japanese, Chinese, Korean and Thai specialities like sushi, sashimi, dim sum, plus more than 20 vegetarian dishes. *UB City (large shopping centre), 24 Vittal Mallya Rd | tel. 080 41 73 88 61*

WHERE TO STAY

BLUE MOON LOG INN

This blue guesthouse with its 20 rooms lies within walking distance of the city's most interesting attractions. It has a kitchen and a coffee shop. The individually-furnished rooms have balconies with lovely views over the city, DVD player, flat-screen TV and wi-fi. *154/9th Sector 6, H.S.R Layout, opposite Lawrence School | tel. 080 25 72 59 99 | www.bluemoongroup.in | Budget*

INSIDER TIP OUR NATIVE VILLAGE ☺

This village lies an hour away from Bangalore and offers, in contrast to the hi-tech city, a holiday on a farm – ideal for families with kids. You can milk the cows, drive an ox-cart, fly kites, go cycling and learn about organic farming. There's even a spa with holistic treatments. *Kodihalli Village, Hessarghatta Rd | tel. 080 41 14 09 09 | www.ournativevillage.com | Moderate*

TAJ WEST END

An oasis of peace with excellent service, whose former patrons include Winston Churchill, Queen Elizabeth II and Queen Silvia of Sweden. Breakfast can be served under the massive 150-year-old rain tree on request. It takes 45 minutes to follow the nature trail through the extensive grounds. In addition, there are two outdoor pools, tennis courts, a spa and

Bangalore Golf Club (18-hole) right next door. *117 rooms | Race Course Rd | tel. 080 66 60 56 60 | www.tajhotels.com | Expensive*

WOODLANDS
This large hotel with 211 rooms, some of them in cottages, was one of the first in Bangalore and it exudes a nostalgic charm. Facilities include a pool and a small beauty salon. *5 Mohan Roy Rd | tel. 080 22 22 51 11 | www.woodlands.in | Budget–Moderate*

INFORMATION

KARNATAKA STATE TOURISM DEVELOPMENT CORPORATION
49 Khanija Bhavan | Race Course Rd | tel. 080 22 35 29 01 | www.karnatakaholidays.net

KARNATAKA TOURISM HOUSE
A One-Stop-Shop | No. 8, Papanna Lane, St Mark's Rd | tel. 080 41 32 92 11

WHERE TO GO

GOLDEN CHARIOT ★
This luxury train decorated in the style of historic maharajas' trains is the most stylish mode of transport for touring and experiencing Karnataka. It also offers an opulent and well-stocked restaurant and bar, plus modern facilities like the wellness, fitness and internet coach. From Bengaluru the Golden Chariot calls at Karnataka's most beautiful destinations on a journey lasting seven days: Mysore, Nagarhole National Park, Belur and Halebid, Shravanabelagola, Hampi, Badami and Pattadakal, before arriving in Goa. *Cost per night approx. 480 $US | www.goldenchariot.com | Expensive*

INSIDER TIP PUTTAPARTHI
(144 C2) (ØØ F7)
Just 160 km (100 mi) north of Bengaluru in the neighbouring state of Andra Pradesh, lies the ashram of the spiritual master Sri Sathya Sai Baba *(www.sathyasai.info)*, who died in 2011. Followers from all over the world still flock to *Prashanti Nilayam*, the 'Abode of Highest Peace'. Accommodation at the ashram which costs only a few rupees, cannot be booked in advance; the *accommodation office* allocates rooms from 8am onwards. Apart from the ashram, there are many hotels in Puttaparthi, such as *Sai Renaissance (31 rooms | By Pass Rd | tel. 08555 2 87 59 14 | www.sairenaissance. com | Budget)* or *Sri Sathya Sai Towers (27 rooms | Main Street | tel. 08555 28 72 70 | www.saitowers.com | Moderate)*. There's a train from Bangalore to Puttaparthi or you can take a taxi from the new airport *(approx. 2 hours | Rs 1,000)*.

HAMPI

(141 E5) (ØØ D6) ★ ● **This is surely one of the most unusual and intriguing places in all India. Hampi was the capital of the Vijayanagar Empire, a kingdom that once covered the whole of South India and stretched as far as Sri Lanka.**
For more than 200 years (1336–1565) Hampi was a thriving city. At its height it would have had a population of some 500,000 – the present-day village of Hampi has only around 10,000 inhabitants. But it's still possible to imagine the city's former splendour; in 1986, it was declared a Unesco World Heritage Site. As well as scattered ruins, within a radius of 26km (16mi) among the bizarre granite rocks south of the Tungabhadra River, lie some well-preserved temples and other impressive buildings.

SIGHTSEEING

The best way to explore the extensive area of the ruined city is on a bike. Temples and monuments are open daily 8.30am–5.30pm.

QUEEN'S BATHROOM

The exterior is less impressive, but the interior compensates with its amazing stucco decoration, vaulted corridor and airy balconies protruding over a 15m × 15m pool. Perfumed water from the lotus-shaped fountains splashed on to the ladies of the court.

ELEPHANT STABLES

An impressive building with numerous domed ceilings that once housed the royal elephants.

HAZARA RAMA TEMPLE

This royal temple is decorated all over with bas-reliefs, which depict scenes from the Hindu epic, the Ramayana.

ROYAL PALACE

In the largest section is a platform with lively bas-reliefs whose themes include hunting, dancing and processions. Just over 100m to the west of that was the audience chamber of the king, complete with pool.

LOTOS MAHAL

This attractive yellow building consists of open pavilions on the ground floor and balconies on the upper floor. Its design is a very impressive example of a successful fusion of Hindu and Islamic architectural elements. The name of the building

Not of this world? Hampi's bizarre combination of temples and giant granite boulders

comes from the beautiful and geometrically arranged arches, which resemble the petals of a lotus flower.

VIRUPAKSHA TEMPLE

The temple is dedicated to Lord Shiva and is still used by devout Hindus. Visible from afar is the nine-storey *gopuram,* entrance tower. If you buy a basket of offerings with flowers and fruit, take care, because the cheeky monkeys are just waiting to snatch it from you.

VITTALA TEMPLE

Dating from the 16th century, this well-preserved temple lies some 2km from the bazaar, Hampi's market, which borders the historic site. In the temple courtyard is the most photographed sight in all of South India: the so-called Stone Chariot, whose wheels once even turned. The outer pillars of the temple are known as the 'Musical Pillars' as they echo when banged. Vittala Temple is considered the pinnacle of Vijayanagar art *(Rs 200; the ticket is also valid for admission to the Zenana complex with the Lotos Mahal and the Elephant Stables).*

FOOD & DRINK

There are numerous small restaurants all around the Hampi bazaar.

GEETHA RIVER VIEW RESTAURANT

This eatery's trump card is its beautiful view of the river. Its various vegetarian dishes such as cashew nut curry taste delicious. *Kampa Bhuppa's Path | Budget*

Top parking spot: the Stone Chariot has been stationary in the courtyard of the Vittala Temple for around 500 years

INSIDER TIP MANGO TREE

This restaurant, situated in a banana plantation on the riverbank, is famous for its cheap and extremely tasty *thalis*. It has a very relaxed atmosphere with many travellers staying the whole afternoon on the ☀ terrace enjoying the view over the river. In the garden is a mango tree with a swing. *500m west of the Virupaksha Temple | tel. 04876 5213 | Budget*

SPORTS & ACTIVITIES

MOPED HIRE
A moped or scooter is a good way of exploring Hampi. Moped shops can be found in the area of the Hampi bazaar, in Kamalapura and in Hospet *(from approx. Rs 150 per day)*.

FUN AND GAMES AFTER THE RICE HARVEST ●
After the rice harvest, between December and March, the farmers around Hampi finally have time to relax and enjoy ox-cart racing and the local version of bullfighting, in which toreros have to capture sweets or money that have been fixed to the animal's head. Other entertainment includes village games with coconuts and also chicken fights(!). Visitors are welcome to join in. Information: *Tourist Information Office Hampi | Hampi Bazaar | tel. 08394 241339*

WHERE TO STAY

In Hampi itself there's plenty of accommodation, but it's all of the basic variety. Those looking for greater comfort are better off heading for Hospet, 13km (8mi) away.

HOTEL MALLIGI
With 160 rooms, this is the best hotel in Hospet. It also has a lovely pool, as well as massage and fitness facilities. *6/143 J. N. Rd | tel. 08394 228101 | www.malligi hotels.com | Expensive*

SHANTI GUEST HOUSE
This charming establishment has 23 rooms, each with a ceiling fan, plus a lush garden overlooking the river, hammocks and bicycles. In the attached restaurant, everything from Nepalese to Thai to Israeli cuisine is served. The atmosphere is friendly and personal. *On the other side of the river, Virupapur Gaddi, Sanapur | tel. 08394 325352 | www.shanthihampi.com | Budget*

LOW BUDGET

▶ Much cheaper than taxis: comfortable air-conditioned Volvo buses leave every 30 minutes from various points in the city for the *Bengaluru International Airport (BIAL Airport)*, which lies 38 km (24 miles) outside. *Rs 125 | Bangalore Metropolitan Transport Corporation (BMTC), Airport Kiosk Information | tel. 077 60991269; Kempegowda Bus Stand | tel. 080 22952314; Shivajinagar Bus Stand | tel. 080 22952321*

▶ A fun and very inexpensive way to explore Hampi's sprawling ruins is by bike. There are several places in Hampi Bazaar that rent out bicycles for between Rs 30–60 per day.

▶ A bed will only cost a few rupees at the station in Bijapur *(Railway Retiring Room and Dorm)*. The accommodation is very clean. Ask the supervisor at the station. The same applies to many Indian stations and airports, the latter with dormitories mostly in the *Domestic Terminal*.

HAMPI

SHIVANANDA
The 23 rooms are simple but clean. While it doesn't have its own restaurant (food can be ordered in), it does have an in-house astrologist. *Next to the bus stop | College Rd, Hospet | tel. 08394 22 07 00 | Moderate*

INFORMATION

TOURIST INFORMATION OFFICE HAMPI
Hampi Bazaar | tel. 08394 24 13 39. They also arrange personal guides, for one day *(Rs 500)* or half-day *(Rs 300)*.

BOOKS & FILMS

▶ **The God of Small Things** – Arundhati Roy tells the story of a family in Kerala, which is torn apart by forbidden love. At the same time, the author depicts the simple life of rural India in all its different guises. Brilliant!

▶ **Plain Tales from the Hills** – A highly amusing classic by Bombay-born Rudyard Kipling, who provides an entertaining insight into the mundane and often decadent lives of British sahibs and memsahibs in the hill stations.

▶ **Best Exotic Marigold Hotel** – This 2012 film with its all-star cast (Judi Dench, Maggie Smith, Bill Nighy) transports the audience into the bustling melee of modern-day India. For a variety of reasons, seven English pensioners converge on this hotel, which promises absolute nirvana. The reality is rather different and is explained by the young manager (Dev Patel from Slumdog Millionaire) in typical Indian fashion: 'I have offered a vision of the future.' With a strong dash of British humour, director John Madden weaves a fine web of interpersonal relationships in a more or less alien world.

▶ **Slumdog Millionaire** – Not every Indian likes Danny Boyle›s blockbuster, which won eight Oscars. After all, with the young Jamal Malik, who takes part in the Indian version of 'Who Wants to be a Millionaire?', he paints a very one-sided picture of Indian poverty, squalor and powerlessness against authority.

▶ **Monsoon Wedding** – This lavish production (2001) directed by Mira Nair uses a wedding to highlight the conflicts between Indian immigrants to America and the older generation back home. At the same time, it captures the wild elation of Indians during the monsoon season, with all the colour and typical Bollywood music and dance routines.

▶ **Lagaan** – This award-winning film (2001) is set in colonial India. British officer Captain Russell (Paul Blackthorne) levies high taxes (lagaan) from the local farmers. If they manage to win a game of cricket, however, he will waive the taxes. Led by Bhuyan (Aamir Khan), the Indian peasants begin training, and, of course, love also features in the game.

You can take dance classes in the cave temple – from Lord Shiva in person

AIHOLE (141 D4) (*∅ D5*)

With around 140 temples, Aihole is the cradle of Indian sacred architecture. The oldest building is thought to be the Lad Khan Temple, dating from the 5th–7th century, with its semi-circular apse. It stands on a raised plinth, and the entire sanctuary is surrounded by a gallery of carvings.

Most of the temples here are dedicated to the Lord Vishnu. Half of them lie within the perimeter wall *(daily 6am–6pm | Rs 100)*. Accommodation is best found in Badami *(44km/28mi southwest of Aihole)*, and the tourist office responsible for Aihole is also there *(in the Hotel Mayura Chalukya, Ramdurga Rd.| tel. 08357 22 00 46)*. 144km (90mi) north-west

BADAMI (141 D4) (*∅ D6*)

This beautifully situated little town (pop. 31,000), around 100km (60mi) from Hampi, is bordered to the east by Agasty-atirtha Lake, which is surrounded by rugged, red sandstone outcrops. The dynasty of the early western Chalukya made Badami its capital and, from the end of the 6th century until the 8th century, created important sacred caves and temples here. Cut into the rock and reached via steps are four old ⭐ *cave temples (daily 6am–6pm | Rs 100)*, whose entrance is marked by columns and brackets. The largest one is Cave 3, which is dedicated to the Lord Vishnu. A particularly eye-catching feature in Cave 1 is the 18-armed Nataraja (Shiva), which depicts 81 different dance moves.

A view over the various temples and ruins of the North Fort is only possible by climbing up a steep flight of steps. The remains of a granary, treasury and observation tower can all be seen. Accommodation options include the *Hotel Rajsangam International (40 rooms | opposite the bus stop, Station Rd | tel. 08357 22 19 91 | www.hotelrajsangaminternational.com | Moderate)*, which has a pool on the  roof terrace and fantastic views of the red cliffs and the cave temples. Or there's the *KSTDC Hotel Mayura Chalukya (10 rooms | Ramdurg Rd | tel. 08357 22 00 46 | Moderate)*, a state-run

most famous building in the city. It is crowned by one of the largest domes in the world – supported by an amazing system of interlocking pendentives. Beneath the dome runs the circular 'whispering gallery', which rebounds an echo eleven times from any given position. Because of the noise levels generated by lots of visitors, it's recommended to come here early in the morning. The Palace Mosque of Ibrahim Rauza with its

Try to find a room with a view of the vast Gol Gumbaz mausoleum

establishment in a peaceful location some distance outside the town centre. It also runs the *Tourist Office*.

BIJAPUR (141 D3) (*☊ D5*)

The former capital (pop. 250,000) of the Adil Shahi kings (1489–1686) reflects the power and influence of the Muslim sultans. It is full of mosques, palaces, forts, towers and a monumental mausoleum. The latter, the ★ *Gol Gumbaz (daily 6.30am–5.30pm | Rs 200, video camera Rs 25)*, was erected in 1659 and is the

mausloeum lies outside the city walls. The tomb was built by Sultan Ibrahim Adil Shah (1580–1627), and contains the graves of the ruler and his wife, Taj Sultana. The mosque *(daily 6am–6pm | Rs 200, video/camera Rs 25)* with its four minarets is thought to have served as the model for the Taj Mahal in Agra.

At the pretty *Swapna Lodge (MG Rd | Budget)* there is a pleasant rooftop restaurant with friendly service. Accommodation is provided by the *Hotel Madhuvan (36 rooms | Station Rd | tel. 08352*

25 55 71 | www.hotelmadhuvan.com | Ex-pensive), complete with garden restaurant, lovely courtyard and fantastic view of the Gol Gumbaz from the ☀ roof terrace. Or the *Sanman (24 rooms | Station Rd, opposite the Gol Gumbaz | tel. 08352 25 18 66 | Budget)*, which offers good value for money. The *Tourist Office* lies behind the hotel *Mayura Adil Shahi, on Station Rd | tel. 08352 5 03 59. 160km (100mi) northwest*

JOG FALLS ● (143 D2) (*m C7*)

The second-highest waterfall in Karnataka (199km/122mi north), which plunges 253m (830ft) into the depths from the 200-m wide bed of the Sharavati River, is undoubtedly the most impressive, primarily because it consists of just one solid column of water that cascades into the gorge over four distinct levels. It's possible to bathe at the base of the falls. For the best views try ☀ *Watkin's Platform* or the ☀ *cliffs* by the *Bombay Bungalow*. Accommodation: *Matthuga Homestay (Talavata, BH Rd (NH 206) | tel. 09880 9 99 75 | www.matthuga.in | Budget)*, 8km (5mi) from the falls, in the middle of an areca plantation (betel nut palms).

PATTADAKAL (141 D4) (*m D5*)

This Unesco World Heritage Site lies 122km (76mi) from Hampi (22km/14mi northeast of Badami) on the Malaprabha River, and its monuments demonstrate just how varied Chalukya architecture was. Pattadakal's ten temples are among the most important early stone temples in India. The largest is the *Virupaksha Temple.* It has an enormous entrance, whose massive columns are decorated with reliefs depicting scenes from the two Hindu epics, Ramayana and Mahabharata. Opposite the temple stands a pavilion with an enormous Nandi bull. The *Mallikarjuna Temple* is similar in design, only a little smaller. The *Papanatha Temple* is a further showpiece, with finely chiselled ceilings and a hall of 16 columns. It's best to stay overnight in Badami. *Daily 6am–6pm | Rs 200.* Information: *Tourist Office Badami* in the *Hotel Mayura Chalukya, Ramdurga Rd | tel. 08357 22 00 46*

MANGALORE

(143 E4) (*m C9*) So far the west coast of Karnataka has remained relatively undiscovered. In this hilly city (pop. 620,000) at the confluence of Gurupura and Nethravathi rivers, something of its heyday as a major port and shipbuilding centre still lingers.

Today, from the new port, 10km (6mi) north of the city centre, they export mainly coffee, pepper and cashew nuts. Along the narrow, often palm-lined streets, stand old houses with roofs of red tile. After waves of conquest and destruction, not much is left in terms of important sights, nevertheless Mangalore makes an excellent base for some interesting excursions.

SIGHTSEEING

KADRI MANJUNATHA TEMPLE

This temple lies 3km (2mi) from the city centre and is thought to be almost 1000 years old. Devotees come here to worship a large *lingam* (stone phallus as a symbol of Shiva) and a 1.6-m (5-ft)high bronze statue of the goddess Lokeshwara with three faces and six arms. The latter is regarded as one of the finest bronze statues in India. At 8am, noon and 8pm INSIDER TIP blessings with fire.

MANGALADEVI TEMPLE

With a dark-red tiled roof dating from the 10th century, this low-rise temple was named after the Malabar princess Mangala Devi, the patron deity of Mangalore. It is said that whoever worships at her statue will be blessed with good fortune and prosperity. Its full name is the Mahatobhara Sri Mangaladevi Temple and it is situated in Bolar, 3km (2mi) southwest of the city.

ST ALOYSIUS COLLEGE CHAPEL

This fine chapel is situated in the heart of the city on Lighthouse Hill. It is visited primarily for its impressive wall and ceiling frescoes that were painted in the late 19th century by the Jesuit priest Antonio Moscheni. They depict biblical scenes, including the Apostle Thomas, who is said to have introduced Christianity to India. *Daily 8–10am, noon–2.30pm, 3.30–6pm*

FOOD & DRINK

DIESEL CAFÉ

Bright and cheerful, with a friendly atmosphere, serving a mix of Italian and Indian dishes. The breakfast servings are particularly lavish. *Collectors Gate, Balmatta Rd | tel. 0824 2 41 06 01 | Budget*

LALITH

This restaurant might be in the basement but it offers an excellent choice of fish and seafood, cold beer and friendly service. *Balmatta Rd | tel. 0824 2 42 67 93 | Budget*

SHOPPING

CAUVERY KARNATAKA ARTS & CRAFTS

In this state-run arts and crafts emporium, the prices for material and items such as statues made of sandalwood and bronze are fixed. *Raj Towers | Balmatta Rd*

BEACHES

INSIDER TIP *Ullal Beach*, a sandy beach 8km (5mi) outside Mangalore, is bordered by the south bank of the Netravati River and is lined with casuarina trees.

ENTERTAINMENT

HOWZZAT SPORTS BAR

This popular venue, a combination of pub and disco, with red walls and red and white club chairs, is in the *Goldfinch Hotel*. The DJ plays a cool mix that would be appreciated by many a Bollywood star. On Saturdays and Sundays *(6.30pm–midnight | Rs 700)* they only admit couples, during the week *(10am–3pm and 6.30pm–midnight | admission free)* also singles. *236/2A1 Bunts Hostel Rd | www.goldfinchhotels.com*

WHERE TO STAY

THE GATEWAY HOTEL 🌿

From this modern 4-star establishment with its 88 bright rooms you can have a lovely view over the fishing port. The hotel has a pool and fitness centre. *Old Port Rd | tel. 0824 6 66 04 20 | www.thegatewayhotels.com | Moderate*

INSIDER TIP SUMMER SANDS BEACH RESORT

Due to its location, this idyllic beach resort is much appreciated by artists and creative types. Huts with tiled roofs housing a total of 80 rooms are dotted around the garden, which has more than 500 palm trees. You can even watch dolphins frolicking from the beach. The hotel also has a pool and rents out bicycles for exploration of the numerous lagoons in the vicinity. *Chotamangalore, Ullal | tel. 0824 24 67 69 02 | www.summer-sands.com | Moderate–Expensive*

HOTEL SURYA
The 18 rooms are nothing special, but this budget hotel does have a quiet location away from the street. *Greens Compound | Balmatta Rd | tel. 0824 2 42 57 36 | Budget*

Cholas. Its facade is richly decorated with life-like sculptures of musicians, dancers and erotic figures. Surrounding the plinth are 644 elephants, each one different from the next. *Daily 7.30am–8.30pm. 165km (103mi) northeast*

Pachyderm procession: 644 small elephants surround the plinth of the Chennakesava Temple

INFORMATION

KSTDC TOURIST INFORMATION
Lighthouse Hill Rd | tel. 0824 2 42 16 92

WHERE TO GO

BELUR (143 F4) (*D8*)
Belur is famous for the magnificent Hoysala Temple complex. The Hoysala Empire ruled most of the modern-day state of Karnataka between 1040 and 1345. On the site the biggest attraction is the ★ *Chennakesava Temple*, which King Vishnuvardhana had built in 1117 to commemorate his victory over the

GOKARNA (143 D2) (*B7*)
Most travellers visit this pilgrimage destination not for the temple but for the legendary ★ *Om Beach*. The beach acquired its name because its curving bays and headlands which create a shape reminiscent of the sacred Om symbol of Hindus and Buddhists. It is followed by another four sandy bays: *Gokarna, Kudle, Half Moon* and *Paradise*. The most deserted are Half Moon and Paradise. Located next to the temples is the pleasant guesthouse *Nimmu House (15 ensuite rooms | Main Bhadra Rd | tel. 08386 25 6730 | Budget)* with a garden and small roof terrace. The terracotta-col-

oured resort of ● 🕓 *Swaswara (Dhoni-bail, Om Beach, Gokarna | tel. 08386 25 71 31 | www.swaswara.com | Expensive)* has 27 villas in local style, each with a large room and yoga deck; they also have an Ayurveda centre, a large pool and a *Meditation Dome*. In the *Namasté Café (Budget)* at Om Beach you can get

At their destination: pilgrims in front of Lord Gomateswara

European food, such as pizza and pasta, as well as felafel. *185km (115mi) north*

HALEBID (143 F3) *(𝄞 D8)*

The old Hoysala capital lies 176km (109mi) northeast of Mangalore. Here it's worth taking a look at the *Hoy-saleswara Temple*, whose walls are richly decorated with a variety of Hindu deities, stylised animals and scenes from the lives of the Hoysala kings.

HASSAN (143 F4) *(𝄞 D8)*

This rather austere town makes a good starting point for visiting nearby Belur, Halebid and Shravanabelagola. Many tourists on this circuit stay at the pleasant garden complex of *Hoysala Village Resort (Belur Rd | tel. 08172 25 67 93 | Expensive)*, that lies 6km (4mi) from Hassan in the direction of Belur and offers 33 rooms in cottages, as well as a pool and spa. Another option is the modern *Hassan Ashok (BM Rd | tel. 08172 26 87 31 | www.has sanashok.com | Moderate)*, which has 36 rooms with rattan furniture, is very well maintained and offers excellent cuisine. Information: *Tourist Office | A.V.K. College Rd | tel. 08172 26 88 62. 160km (100mi) east*

MURUDESHWAR (143 D2) *(𝄞 B7)*

For one of the best dive sites in South India, travel north along the coast from Mangalore for about 150km (90mi). From *Murudeshwar* near Bhatka, there's great diving and snorkelling in the amazing underwater world (wrecks included) off the small island of INSIDER TIP *Net-rani (Pigeon Island)*. Contact PADI certified *Dreamz Diving | Rs 4000–5000 per dive, Rs 2500 for snorkelling | tel. 097 40 75 24 80 and tel. 093 26 15 13 00 | www.dreamzdiving.com*

SHRAVANABELAGOLA ★
(144 A4) *(𝄞 D9)*

This important place of pilgrimage for the Jains is located 125km (78mi) east of Mangalore. At Shravanabelagola stands the colossal, monolithic statue of Lord Gomateswara, a Jain deity. The 17-m (56-ft) high, naked figure carved from granite, with its extra long arms symbolising wisdom, can be seen from up to 30km (18mi) away. To get to the top of Vindhyagiri Hill you can either climb the 614 steps or have yourself carried up in a litter. Every twelve years (the last time was in 2005), ceremonies lasting several days are performed in honour of Lord Gomateswara. *Free admission, donations welcome.* Information: *Tourist Office, at the foot of Vindhyagiri Hill*

MYSORE

(144 A5) *(ɷ D9)* **This former capital of the princely state (pop. 3 million) has a majestic aura. Here the pace is much more relaxed than in Bengaluru.**

There's something magical about the broad, tree-lined avenues, villas with pink bougainvillea spilling from their gardens and the parks surrounding the shining white *Lalith Mahal Palace* – today a hotel. Even if the many souvenir shops and bland new-builds rather dull the image, in the evening, when the sun no longer illuminates the facades so mercilessly, Mysore suddenly basks again in its ageless beauty.

SIGHTSEEING

CHAMUNDI HILL ☙

Some 1000 steps lead to the top of this 1062-m (3484-ft) high hill, which is crowned by the Sri Chamundeswari Temple with its richly decorated *gopuram* (entrance tower). A little further down stands the 4.8-m (16-ft) high Nandi Bull, which was hewn out of black granite in 1659.

JAYACHAMARAJENDRA ART GALLERY

This gallery contains precious treasures of the maharajas, including antique furniture, old musical instruments and figures of ivory and sandalwood. It is housed in the Jagan Mohan Palace, west of the enormous Maharaja's Palace. *Daily 8.30am–5.30pm | Rs 15*

MYSORE PALACE ★

The focal point of the city is the magnificent Maharaja's Palace *(Amba Vilas)*, built in Indo-Sarenic style and richly adorned with domes, towers, arches and colonnades. It was built in 1912 to replace the previous palace from 1897 that had burned down, and is a treasure trove of exquisite carvings, works of art from around the world, old paintings and a throne of pure gold. During festivals, the palace is illuminated in the evening by 96,000 light bulbs. *Daily 10am–5.30pm | Rs 200 | admission through the south gateway, Purandara Dasa Rd | www.mysorepalace.org*

FOOD & DRINK

EDELWEISS

Café serving Austrian specialities. The kitchen is open so guests can watch as their schnitzel, etc, is being prepared. They also serve really good coffee. *2681/1 9th Cross, Adipampa Rd, V.V. Mohalla | tel. 0821 6 45 24 48 | Budget*

GANESH

Very reasonably priced *dosas,* filled with vegetables and potatoes. *Opposite the Central Bus Stand | Budget*

OM SHANTI

In addition to serving dishes from all over the world, the speciality of this restaurant is its cheap but tasty *thalis. Hotel Siddharta | Guest House Rd | tel. 0821 2 52 28 88 | Budget*

SHOPPING

Mysore is famous for its extravagant silks, sandalwood, rosewood carvings and wooden toys, as well as its pictures using natural colours and gold leaf depicting scenes from Hindu mythology.

MYSORE

CAUVERY ARTS & CRAFTS EMPORIUM

Here, you will find applied arts, many items made of sandalwood and also the authentic sandalwood powder. In addition, high-quality products made of brass and the famous Mysore pictures. All at fixed prices. *Sayyaji Rao Rd*

INSIDER TIP DEVARAJA FRUIT & VEGETABLE MARKET ●

This wonderful market appeals to all the senses in equal measure. In the fruit hall there's the sweet smell of mangos and bananas, while in the flower hall you'll be almost overwhelmed by the fragrance of thousands of jasmine flowers and roses. A visual feast is provided by the tall, conical mounds of coloured powder *(kumkum). Daily 6am–8.30pm | Sayyaji Rao Rd*

GOVERNMENT SILK FACTORY

Mysore is renowned for its beautiful silk. You can go right to the source, to a factory, and watch weavers as they produce the finest silk saris with ornamental trims. In the shop, apart from saris, you can buy precious fabrics in every imaginable colour and pattern, by the metre and at factory prices. *Mon–Sat 10am–noon and 2–4pm | Mananthody Rd*

SANDALWOOD OIL FACTORY

What a scent! This is where the sandalwood oil is extracted, in order to make perfume. They also sell soap, joss sticks, cosmetics and Ayurvedic products made of sandalwood, as well as sandalwood carvings. *Mon–Sat 9–11am and 2–4pm | Manandavady Rd*

ENTERTAINMENT

HIGH OCTANE

The cool crowd parties at this fashionable club, with alternating themes directed by popular DJs and graphic light effects projected onto the walls. Admission for couples only. *2820 8th Cross Adipampa Rd, V.V. Mohalla | www.highoctanemys.com*

OPIUM

This pub in the Pai Vista Hotel is well-known for its loud heavy-rock music and the numerous portraits of rock stars decorating the walls. *35 A Bn Rd*

WHERE TO STAY

GREEN HOTEL

This hotel has a total of 31 rooms, all with balcony and stylish wooden furniture. The best rooms are in the former Princess Palace, the cheaper ones in the new annexe. Standing in extensive grounds, it is run on environmentally friendly lines, with some of the profits going to environmental projects. *Chittaranjan Palace | 2270 Vinoba Rd, Jayalakshmipuram | tel. 0821 4 25 50 00 | www.greenhotelindia. com | Moderate*

LALITHA MAHAL PALACE

This former palace, which the vegetarian maharaja had built specially for his meat-eating guests, has often been used as a film set. The four-poster beds and antique furniture in each of the 54 rooms and suites convey a right-royal feeling. *Siddarth Nagar | tel. 0821 2 52 61 00 | www.lalithamahalpalace.in | Expensive*

RITZ HOTEL

It doesn't quite live up to its name – this particular establishment is a simple budget hotel. Be that as it may, it's been on the go for 60 years, has four rooms but a lot of character, a shady courtyard and is not far from the bus station. *Bangalore-Nilgiri Rd | tel. 0821 2 42 26 68 | Budget*

TOURIST RECEPTION CENTRE
Old Exhibition Building | Irwin Rd | tel. 0821 2 42 20 96

WHERE TO GO

NAGARHOLE NATIONAL PARK ★
(143 F5) *(ΩΩ D9)*
Some 80km (50mi) south of Mysore lies the Nagarhole National Park, the former hunting grounds of the Maharajas of Mysore. Today, monkeys do their acrobatics in trees and the park provides a habitat for more than 200 elephants, 100 tigers and over 50 leopards. There's lots for visitors to do in the park: jeep safaris, boat trips on the River Kabini, kayak and pedal boat tours, elephant rides and hikes. A lovely place to stay is the *Kabini River Lodge (Karapura, Nissana Beltur Post | tel. 08228 26 44 02* or through *Jungle Lodges & Resorts Ltd. | Bengaluru | tel. 080 40 55 40 55 | www. junglelodges.com | Expensive)* with its 14 colonial-style double rooms, ten twin-bedded cottages in wooded surroundings and six tented cottages.

SRIRANGAPATNA (144 A5) *(ΩΩ D9)*
This 5-km long and 1-km wide island lies 14km (8mi) northeast of Mysore, surrounded by the Kaveri River (access via bridge). The sights of this former capital of the Wodeyar kings and stronghold of Tipu Sultan, the legendary 'Tiger of Mysore', can best be explored by rented bicycle. The *Old Fortress (daily 9am–5pm | Rs 50)* includes Captain Bailey's Dungeon, where British soldiers were held captive by Tipu Sultan. Within the fortress stands the *Sri Ranganathaswamy Temple (daily 8am–2pm and 4–7pm)* with its five-storey entrance gateway. Quite unassuming from the outside is the *Daria Daulat Bagh (Sat–Thu 9am–5pm | Rs 100)*, the 18th-century, two-storey summer palace of Tipu Sultan, made entirely of teak and notable for its murals and carved pillars. The Gumbaz Mausoleum *(Sat–Thu 8am–6.30pm | free admission)* with its white dome is the resting place of the sultan's family.

Peaceful times in Nagarhole National Park, the former hunting ground of the maharajas

TAMIL NADU

Tamil Nadu, a world of wonder: this magical mix of nature and culture, of beaches, green hill stations and historical sites, has always enthralled travellers. Clocks work differently here, notions of time matter less.

Magnificent temples adorn every village. In Madurai the temple contains amazingly decorated entrance towers, or *gopuram,* the sea temples in Mamallapuram are subject to the laws of eternal wave action. Tamil Nadu can also boast of having the most World Heritage Sites. Three of the five sites are located in Thanjavur, the other two in Chennai and Nilgiri.

Even in prehistoric times, people were settling in the area of the present-day state of Tamil Nadu, which emerged out of the province of Madras in 1969. With an area of just over 50,000 sq. mi. the state is about the same size as Greece. The art and culture of this region is among the oldest in the world. One of the world's longest surviving classical languages, the Tamil language was written down 5000 years ago and first spoken long before that. Tamil Nadu can be regarded as one of the last remaining places on earth with a continuing classical culture. The ancient Dravidian heritage is still very much alive; history doesn't just refer to the dim distant past, but it lives on in music and dance, in the palaces and temples where ancient beliefs continue to be practised.

Since time immemorial, each day has begun with women, in front of their

Photo: Kanyakumari

Sea temples and hill stations, ancient cultures and beautiful landscapes offer a unique range of attractions

houses, painting kolams – intricate stylised patterns made with coloured rice powder. This strong sense of creativity is also manifest in the film industry, for which the state is famous. 'There's more to cinema than Bollywood', they say. Outsized movie posters of film heroes and heroines adorn the walls of houses in every town, in every village. And the refined culture of Tamil Nadu has even left its mark on the cuisine. Among connoisseurs, the region of Chettinad is considered the home of India's gourmet chefs,

its cuisine incorporating a variety of culinary influences from across the continent. Delicious, delicately spiced dishes of mutton, chicken and fish are prepared here, and the art of making excellent coffee has been perfected.

To enjoy the pleasures of high society, the British colonial masters took to their chic *hill stations* like Ooty, also known as Udhagamandalam. Today's influx will discover an amazing amount to see and do: surrounded by the Bay of Bengal with its palm-lined beaches in the east, the Nil-

In front of Chennai station as the elephant-headed Ganesh looks on

giri Mountains (part of the Western Ghats) in the west, the Indian Ocean in the south and the Deccan Plateau in the north, Tamil Nadu offers lots of variety. When not on the palm beaches plunging into the temptingly warm waters of the Indian Ocean, active holidaymakers go trekking, fishing, canoeing, or play golf. While the total of 900km (560mi) of beaches along Tamil Nadu's Coromandel Coast might not be as well-known as those in Goa or Kerala, they do have their own special character. Much was destroyed by the 2004 tsunami, but there's little evidence of that disaster today. Had it occurred 2000 years ago it would have been carved in stone for all eternity – just like so many other events in Tamil Nadu's history.

CHENNAI (MADRAS)

MAP INSIDE BACK COVER
(145 F4) (*M H8*) The climate in and around Tamil Nadu's capital, Chennai (pop. 4.9 million), is described as 'hot, hotter, the hottest'.

That may be something of an exaggeration, as the waters of the Bay of Bengal 'only' get as warm as 32°C (90°F). Alongside the booming IT sector, the city once called Madras, the fourth-largest metropolis in India, can be proud of a history stretching back almost 2000 years. A vivid example of this rich past is the district of *Mylapore*. Beside the Hindu temple of Kapaleeshwarar and Chennai's oldest place of Christian worship, Luz

Church, stands the Basilica San Thome – one of three churches worldwide said to contain the grave of one of the Twelve Apostles. An equally exciting mixture of temples, churches and colonial buildings such as the High Court and the imposing Post Office, thrives in the business district of *George Town.* While Mumbai is well ahead as a producer of Bollywood mov-ies, Chennai has made a big name for itself as the centre of the Tamil film industry – 'Kollywood' as they call it.

WHERE TO START?
Government Museum in Eg-more: In *Egmore,* at the heart of Chennai, near the main station and the bus terminals, you will find the Government Museum. From here, buses of the *Metropolitan Transportation Corporation (www.mtcbus.org)* nos. 10 and 11 will take you right through the city, and are extremely cheap. The MTC also goes to Fort St George at Marina Beach, to San Thome Basilica and the neighbouring Kapaleeshwarar Temple.

SIGHTSEEING

FORT ST GEORGE
This stately fortress is very well preserved. Dating from the 17th century, it was originally built by the Portuguese and later protected the British trading outpost of Chennai. The white fort also contains the oldest Anglican church in India, St Mary's, which was built in 1680. Displays inside the *Fort Museum* include interesting exhibits from the time of the East India Company: uniforms, weapons and medals. In the neighbouring cemetery stand the oldest British gravestones in India. *Sat–Thu 9.30am–5pm | Rs 100 | Kamarajar Salai | south George Town*

GOVERNMENT MUSEUM CHENNAI
With its palace-like main building, this red-coloured museum is one of the oldest in the country. It consists of a total of

★ **Kapaleeshwarar Temple**
This temple of Shiva in Chennai has a splendid, colourful gopuram → p. 98

★ **Fisherman's Cove**
A smart resort on the picture-postcard Covelong Beach → p. 101

★ **Mamallapuram**
Amazing place with sea temples, caves and beautiful rock reliefs → p. 103

★ **Puducherry**
The white city exudes French charm → p. 104

★ **Sri Meenakshi Temple**
Twelve gopuram and a total of 33 million figures adorn South India's largest temple complex in Madurai. It's worth staying to see the night ceremony → p. 105

★ **Rock Fort**
Like a swallow's nest, castle and temple cling to their rocky eyrie high above Tiruchirappalli → p. 110

★ **Udhagamandalam**
Very British: with its English architecture, Ooty or Ootacamund was considered the Queen of hill stations → p. 110

MARCO POLO HIGHLIGHTS

six buildings dotted around a park, each one devoted to a different theme. The site is also home to the *National Art Gallery*, the *Contemporary Art Gallery*, the *Bronze Gallery* and the *Museum of Childhood*. *Sat–Thu 9.30am–5pm | Rs 250,*

LOW BUDGET

▶ You can eat well and cheaply in restaurants, where there are no tables or chairs and you just have a plate in your hand. They are called *kaiyendhi bhavans* in Tamil Nadu and in Kerala they're known as *thattu kadai*. They usually serve typical South Indian snacks such as *idlis, dosas* and *puris*. You can eat at least as cheaply in the *dhabas*, simple roadside restaurants of North Indian origin. Their sweet *chai*, which is prepared over a charcoal fire, and *chicken tikka masala* (spiced chicken) are particularly popular.

▶ You can get around cheaply in Puducherry. Large motor-rickshaws *(4-wheelers)* for max. 8 people stop everywhere on request. The route goes along a 10-km (6-mi) ring road around the city and each passenger pays 5 rupees.

▶ In Mysore there are lots of ☺ cycle rickshaws. This environmentally friendly and cheap way of getting round all the sights or going from point A to point B also supports a dying profession.

▶ Clean beds for next-to-nothing in six *Railway Retiring Rooms* at Thanjavur railway station.

camera Rs 200, video camera Rs 250 | Pantheon Rd, Egmore | www.chennai museum.org

HORTICULTURAL GARDEN
A wonderfully green, cool oasis at the heart of the city, this large, 22-acre park is planted with rare trees, shrubs, bonsais and flowerbeds. *Fri–Wed 8.30am–12.30pm, 1.30–5.30pm | admission free | Cathedral Rd*

KAPALEESHWARAR TEMPLE ★
This temple to Shiva, full of sacred statues, including bronze effigies of the 63 Shaivate saints, boasts a splendid, colourful tower, the 37-m (121-ft) high *gopuram*. The original temple, thought to date from the 7th century, was destroyed by the Portuguese; the present complex is only about 300 years old. Non-Hindus are welcome to step inside the temple courtyard. *Daily 6–11.30am and 4–8pm | camera Rs 25 | Kutchery Rd, Mylapore*

LUZ CHURCH
The oldest church in Chennai, also known as 'Our Dear Lady of Light' or 'Kaatu Kovil', was erected by Franciscans in 1516. It is said that once, when a ship got into difficulties during a storm, the crew saw a light on the shore that pointed the way to safety. Some years later, to give thanks the Portuguese built a church at the same spot. *Luz Church Rd, Mylapore*

SAN THOME BASILICA (ST THOMAS MOUNT CHURCH)
According to tradition, the Apostle Thomas was martyred on the 160 steps which lead up to the top of the hill. In 1523 the Portuguese erected a small church on the site. Both this and a later church crumbled, and it wasn't until 1896 that the white cathedral was built; it was accorded the status of a basilica in 1956. In

the crypt, a statue of the apostle lies in a glass coffin over the grave. *Daily 6am–8pm | Santhome High Rd, Mylapore | www.santhomechurch.com*

FOOD & DRINK

INSIDER TIP AMETHYST CAFÉ

This café belongs to a gallery full of antiquities, paintings and old photographs,

804 Mount Rd | tel. 044 28 52 51 09 | www.annalakshmichennai.com | Expensive

SARAVANABHAVAN

An affordable restaurant which serves up a good range of vegetarian dishes, both Chinese and South Indian; delicious *thalis in particular. Vadapalani Andavar, Koil Street | tel. 044 24 80 25 77 | www.saravanabhavan.com | Budget*

Family outing Indian style – scooter, father, mother, child

housed in a lovely old villa. You eat outside in the garden among giant ferns and palm trees. The menu has mainly Italian dishes. A lovely, green oasis in the heart of the city. *Padmavathi Rd | tel. 044 45 99 16 27 | Moderate*

ANNALAKSHMI

Purely vegetarian, this restaurant is a project sponsored by the *Temple of Fine Arts International,* which combines art, cuisine, dance and theatre and so it also serves as a gallery of art and applied art.

SHOPPING

Chennai's main shopping areas are *Parry's Corner* and *Anna Salai.*

CENTRAL COTTAGE INDUSTRIES EMPORIUM

This state-run emporium for Indian arts and crafts, material, saris, jewellery and much more offers good quality at fixed prices. *672, Temple Towers, Anna Salai, Nandanam | www.cottageemporiumindia.com*

CHENNAI (MADRAS)

PLANET M
Unbeatable prices in this shop, which is a real eldorado for all music and film fans. It has branches in other cities of South India, as well as three in Chennai: *3rd Avenue Anna Nagar; 113 Kutchery Rd, Mylapore; A 9 Abirami, Mega Mall, Kilpauk*

SPORTS & ACTIVITIES

INSIDER TIP DANCE SHOWS
Bharatanatyam, a solo dance from Tamil Nadu, is one of eight classical Indian dance styles that by their form of expression relate certain religious episodes from Hindu mythology. The dance's roots lie in South Indian temple culture. There's an opportunity to watch students of Bharatanatyam by visiting the *Kalakshetra School of Dance. Mon–Fri 10–11.30am | Rs 200 | Thiruvanmiyur | tel. 044 24521169 | www.kalakshetra.in*

BEACHES IN THE VICINITY
All beaches, from north to south **(145 F4)** *(m H8–9)*

MARINA BEACH
The city of Chennai's wide and 12-km (7-mi) long beach stretches from Fort St George in the north to Velankanni Church in the south. Numerous stone statues of famous politicians, including Mahatma Gandhi, line the coast road. A stroll along the beach will take in a number of colonial buildings such as the Senate House, the University Library and the Chepauk Palace. Swimming is not recommended as the water isn't clean enough.

ELLIOT'S BEACH
At the southern end of Marina Beach in Chennai, the curving Elliot's Beach has been used as a location for a number of Tamil films. The sand and water here are clean, the waves are perfect for surfers and there is a choice of restaurants for sustenance.

The Kalakshetra School of Dance trains not just dancers but also musicians

COVELONG BEACH

Visitors to this broad, palm-fringed beach, situated just 40km (25mi) south of Chennai, can enjoy the added attraction of some small fishing villages – it's an almost untouched idyll. All that lies on the beautiful beach itself is the ⭐ *Fisherman's Cove (Covelong Beach | tel. 044 67 41 33 33 | www.tajhotels.com | Expensive)*. It has 88 rooms, some in cottages, good yoga courses and, amongst other restaurants, the romantic *Bay View Point* right on the water's edge.

ENTERTAINMENT

When it comes to nightlife, Chennai has quite a lot to offer. However, all clubs and bars have to close by midnight so places open up correspondingly early.

BIKE & BARREL RESTOBAR

In this comfy pub/bar, beer is served straight from the barrel, and a 1946 Norton Classic motorcycle hangs from the ceiling. At weekends there is a dress code; anyone looking scruffy will be turned away. *Daily 11.30am–11.30pm | 115 Residency Towers | Sir Theagaraya Rd | www.theresidency.com*

PASHA

The best-known nightclub in the city is at the *Park Hotel*. A sultry, oriental atmosphere, hundreds of mirrors reflecting the dance floors and seating, cushions and candles. Admission for couples only. *Rs 1000 | 601 Anna Salai | www.theparkhotels.com*

SATHYAM CINEMAS ●

Cinema in India is a thrilling experience. This multiplex in the city centre has six different theatres, the largest of which seats 948 people; they show international movies as well as Hindi productions à la Bollywood, also in 3-D versions. In addition: vegetarian restaurant, amusement arcade. *8 Thiruvika Rd | tel. 044 42 24 42 24 | www.sathyamcinemas.com*

WHERE TO STAY

HOTEL PANDIAN

It hardly gets more central than this: in two minutes you're at the Egmore Railway Station, and the Central Railway Station is just a five-minute taxi ride away. The rooms are clean and quiet, the main sound being the call of the muezzin from the nearby mosque. Equipped with internet café *(7am–11pm)*. *90 rooms | 15 Kenneth Lane, Egmore | tel. 044 28 19 10 10 | www.hotelpandian.com | Budget–Moderate*

NEW VICTORIA

This hotel has 50 rooms in total, is just 200m from the station and offers excellent value for money. It has a restaurant serving international cuisine, as well as a bar. *3 Kenneth Lane | tel. 044 28 19 36 38 | www.empeehotels.com | Expensive*

`INSIDER TIP` **NEW WOODLANDS HOTEL**

The walls of this centrally located hotel are adorned with images of the Hindu epics. It has an outdoor pool, a beauty salon, two vegetarian restaurants (no alcohol), and is a favourite with international travellers. *175 rooms, some in cottages | 72–75 Dr Radhakrishnan Rd, Mylapore | tel. 044 28 11 31 11 | www.new woodlands.com | Moderate*

INFORMATION

Sightseeing tours through *Tamil Nadu Tourism Development Corporation (TTDC): half-day Chennai (1.30–6.30pm) in air-conditioned bus | Rs 250–300; Hop-on-hop-off tour Chennai/Mamallapuram | Rs 225 | Mon–Fri 10am–5.55pm, Sat/Sun 9am/10am–5.55pm/6.40pm | fees for museums extra.* All tours start at *Tamil Nadu Tourism Complex | 2 Wallajah Rd | tel. 044 25 36 83 58 | www.tamilnadu tourism.org*

INDIA TOURISM OFFICE
154 Anna Salai | tel. 044 28 46 02 85

WHERE TO GO

CHIDAMBARAM (145 E6) (*⟋ H10*)

Like Madurai, the small city of Chidambaram (pop. 82,000) was built around its temple. Between 907 and 1310 this was the capital of the important Chola Empire. Today, it's mainly students from the Annamalai University who throng the streets and bustling market of the old city centre. The main attraction is the *Nataraja Temple (daily 4am–noon and 4–9pm)*. Dating from the 11th century, this 40-acre temple precinct with its 1000-columned hall, is venerated as one of the holiest shrines in South India. The roof is gilded, and the four gopuram soar to a height of 42m (140ft). It is said that the lamps on the towers aided mariners with navigation. Non-Hindus are allowed to enter the holy of holies. At noon and again at 6pm, Nataraja, the statue of the dancing Shiva, is carried around in a litter. The *Hotel Saradharam (19 Venugopal Pillai Street | tel. 04144 22 13 36 | www.ho telsaradharam.co.in | Moderate)* has 45 spacious rooms, some with balcony or terrace. It sounds grander than it actually is: the *Grand Palace Stay (12 Railway Feeder Rd, opposite the station | tel. 04144 23 99 77 | www.grandpalacestay. com | Budget)* with its futuristic facade and small garden has just 21 rooms, two restaurants (one of them vegetarian), a bar and free internet. Information: *Railway Feeder Rd | tel. 04144 25 36 83 58. 232km (144mi) south*

`INSIDER TIP` **DAKSHINACHITRA** ●
(145 F4) (*⟋ H8*)

Some 25km (16mi) south of Chennai lies this model village with traditional houses from all over South India. Demonstrations of art and handicrafts offer a fascinating insight into daily life. You can have mehndi patterns applied to your hands and a parrot will tell your fortune. *Wed–Mon 10am–6pm | Rs 175 | East Coast Rd, Muttukadu | www.dakshina chitra.net*

KANCHIPURAM (145 E4) (*⟋ G9*)

Kanchipuram (pop. 220,000) is considered to have been an example for the fusion of different religions. Of the more than 1000 places of worship it once had, 126 still remain. The *Vaikuntha Perumal Temple* was built in the 7th century by the Pallava king, Nandhivarman. Located in the temple tower are unique images of the Lord Vishnu, seated, standing and recumbent. Dating from the 8th century, the sandstone *Kailasanathar Temple* has a main central shrine with 58 small

All over Mamallapuram: stone masons and the sound of hammer and chisel

shrines surrounding it. Kanchipuram is famous for its high quality silk saris. It's well worth visiting the *Weaver's Service Center | Railway Station Rd*.

Recommended accommodation includes the *MM Hotel (65 Nellukkara Street | tel. 044 27 22 72 50 | www.mmhotels.com | Budget–Moderate):* the 48 rooms are clean and nicely furnished and the restaurant is right next-door. With its 33 rooms, the *Baboo Surya Hotel (85 East Raja Street | tel. 0412 27 22 25 55 | www. hotelbaboosoorya.com | Budget–Moderate)* has been completely renovated. It offers varied cuisine, and cocktails are mixed at the bar. Information: *at the fort. 75km (47mi) southwest*

MAMALLAPURAM (MAHABALIPURAM)
★ ● (145 F4) (*H9*)

Just 55km (34mi) south of Chennai, in the small town of the same name (pop. 13,400), lies the incomparable Unesco World Heritage Site of Mamallapuram. The art of stonemasonry has been preserved here and all over town you can

hear the sound of hammer and chisel. In order for the magic of this former capital of the Pallava kings and their temple to fully sink in, you need to take your time. It is best to hire a bicycle *(Rs 30 per day)*. The *Shore Temple (admission Rs 250),* a sea temple with twin shrines dating from the 7th century, stands majestically over the shore. Of the nine cave temples, the Krishna Cave is especially worth seeing, on account of its realistic depictions. The five temple chariots, *rathas,* were hewn as monoliths from a single block of stone, though they have no wheels. Among the chariots stands a life-sized elephant. *Arjuna's Penance* is one of the largest and most beautiful bas-reliefs in the world (27m × 9 m), full of elephants, celestial beings and people.

Krishna's Butterball was created by nature. This giant block of granite weighing many tons seems to defy the laws of gravity by not rolling down the steep incline on which it is perched.

Because of its relaxing atmosphere, international airline crews like to stay at the INSIDER TIP *Ideal Beach Resort (164 Devenera Village | tel. 044 2 44 95 16 14 | www.idealresort.com | Moderate)*. Its red bungalows with a total of 69 rooms stand in a large garden, together with an Ayurveda centre, beauty salon, tennis courts and pool. The 49 bright rooms at the ☆ *Sea Breeze (tel. 044 27 44 30 35 | Budget–Moderate)* might be basic, but the hotel has beautiful views of the Shore Temple. It also has a pool, garden restaurant and Ayurveda centre. Information: *Tourist Information Office | East Raja Street | tel. 044 27 44 22 32*

MANGROVE PICHAVARAM FOREST ●
(147 F2) (*ᗌ G10*)

Away from civilisation, a boat ride takes you through the mangroves. The *Pichavaram Forest*, 13km (8mi) east of Chidambaram, covers an area of 4.25 sq. mi. and is, after Sundarbans (near Calcutta), the second largest mangrove forest in the world. It provides a habitat for a variety of birds including cormorants, storks, ibis and pelicans; a total of 144 species have been identified. Motorboat and rowing boat tours are offered (someone else does the rowing). *Tours lasting 2, 4 and 6 hours | from Rs 200 with additional Rs 5 entrance | Tourist Office Chidambaram | Railway Feeder Rd | Boat Dept. | tel. 04144 29 08 60*

PUDUCHERRY (PONDICHERRY) ★
(147 F1) (*ᗌ G–H 9–10*)

This city (pop. 800,000) is divided into two by a canal. On one side stand modern, ordinary-looking buildings, on the other the 'White City', which exudes a charm befitting the former capital of French India. Just 8km (5mi) to the south, the secluded *Paradise Beach* can be reached by boat across a small river from Chunnambar Resort. Along the seafront promenade of *Goubert Salai* the great statesman Mahatma Gandhi is honoured with a 4-m high statue.

The *Puducherry Government Museum (Tue–Sun 10am–5pm)* in St Louis Street displays a collection of rare bronze and stone sculptures from the Pallava and Chola dynasties, as well as the bed of the governor general, François Dupleix.

In ● *La Boutique d'Auroville (Jawaharlal Nehru Street)* you can purchase a brochure (Rs 40) to find out about INSIDER TIP *Auroville (www.auroville. org | 10km (6 miles) north of Puducherry)* and the *Sri Aurobindo Ashram*. Lots of lovely items produced at the ashram are also available to buy there. The largest spiritual centre in India was founded in 1968 by Mira Alfassa, known as 'The Mother', who was successor to the philosopher Sri Aurobindo. Her vision was to have a universal city of spiritual freedom that could accommodate 50,000 people. At the moment, around 2200 people from 47 countries live on the site, which covers an area of 10 sq. mi. Its focal point is the 29-m (95-ft) high *Matri Mandir*, a meditation centre beneath a golden dome. At the *Visitor's Centre (daily 9.30am–12.30pm and 2–4pm | tel. 0413 2 62 22 39)* you can find out about yoga courses and investigate basic accommodation, which costs from approx. Rs 350; this includes laundry, bicycle hire and board. Information is also available in Puducherry from very helpful and competent staff: *Goubert Ave (coast road) | tel. 0413 2 33 94 97.*

Besides the ashram, ☺ *The Dune Eco Beach Village (Pudhukuppam, Keelputhupet | booking through Pondicherry University | tel. 0413 2 65 57 51 | www.thedune hotel.com | Moderate)*, some 15km (9mi) from Puducherry, provides not altogether conventional accommodation. This artists' village with 30 villas and 20 rooms has a pool, an organic farm, tennis courts and spa in which Ayurvedic treatments and yoga are offered. *165km (103mi) south*

MADURAI

(147 D4) (∅ F11) Everything in this 2500-year-old city (pop. 1.2 million) on the Vaigai River revolves around the Sri Meenakshi Temple complex.

The street plan of Madurai is aligned with the temple *gopuram*. Modest, new buildings contrast sharply with the opulent splendour of the religious complex, but the sweet aroma that wafts through the city provides enough in the way of compensation: Madurai is famous for its jasmine flowers, which are offered for sale on every street corner. In the Old Town, the narrow alleyways, the bazaar and the pedestrian zone are always a hive of activity. Even as capital of the Pandya Dynasty, who ruled from here for almost a thousand years until the 10th century,

Madurai was both a thriving commercial centre and seat of three literary academies.

SIGHTSEEING

GANDHI MEMORIAL MUSEUM

This museum is dedicated to the great philosopher and freedom fighter Mahatma Gandhi (1869–1948). Besides a large photographic exhibition on his life, numerous anti-British writings are on display. Other exhibits include some of Gandhi's few personal belongings, such as the blood-spattered *dhoti* he was wearing when assassinated. *Daily 10am–1pm and 2–5.30pm | free admission, camera Rs 50 | Rani Mangammal Palace | www.gandhimmm.org*

SRI MEENAKSHI SUNDARESHWARAR TEMPLE ★

Considered the biggest architectural marvel in all South India, this is dedicated to Lord Shiva in his incarnation as

One, two, three … oh forget it! 33 million figures are said to adorn the Sri Meenakshi Temple

Sundareshwarar and his wife Parvati in her incarnation as Meenakshi. Visible from afar, the four *gopuram*, which soar up to 46m (151ft) in height, dominate the city. There is actually a total of 12 *gopuram* within the temple precinct; the renovated towers are adorned with an unbelievable number of colourful deities and demons, said to number some 33 million in all. Since it was first erected in 1560, the complex in Madurai's Old Town has continuously expanded to the size it is today, namely 16 acres. It is considered a perfect example of Dravidian architecture. A particular highlight is the 1000-columned hall. Next door is an art museum containing statues of all the Hindu gods. For non-Hindus there is no admission to the Meenakshi shrine. During the nightly *Arathi Ceremony* between 9 and 9.30pm the statue of Shiva is carried through the temple on a silver litter to join Parvati. *Daily 5am–12.30pm and 4–9.30pm | Rs 50, camera Rs 30, video not allowed, admission to art museum Rs 10 | www.maduraimeenakshi.org*

THIRUMALAI NAYAK PALACE

Located about 1.5km/1mi from the Meenakshi Temple, this palace was built in 1636 for the ruler Thirumalai Nayak. An imposing building, it is renowned for the richly carved decoration in its dome and arches, as well as for its enormous 20-m(66-ft) high white columns. The *Swargavilasa* (Celestial Pavilion) measures 75m × 52m (245ft × 170ft), its central dome floating 25m (82ft) above the floor. A sound & light show *(in English at 6.45pm)* brings Thirumalai Nayak, one of the most popular Madurai kings, back to life. *Daily 9am–1pm and 2–5pm | Rs 50, camera/video Rs 100*

FOOD & DRINK

INSIDER TIP AARATHY

This restaurant in the front garden of the Aarathy Hotel seats around 25 people and serves purely vegetarian dishes such as *thalis*; but the big draw is the feeding of the temple elephant. Twice a day, at 6.30am and 5pm, the pachyderm strolls past and allows himself to be showered by the guests with *idlis* (rice cakes), *cha patis* and fruit. *9 Perumal Koil | West Mada Street | tel. 0452 2 33 15 71 | Budget*

ANNA MEENAKSHI

Vegetarian restaurant with a very reasonably priced menu, including delicious *thalis* authentically served on banana leaves. *West Perumal Maistry Street | Budget*

SURYA

The Surya Restaurant serves vegetarian, Indian-Chinese dishes and from its roof terrace you can also enjoy priceless views of the illuminated Meenakshi Temple. *Approx. 10 min from the temple by auto-rickshaw, Hotel Supreme | 110 West Perumal Maistry Street | tel. 0452 2 34 31 51 | www.supremehotels.com | Moderate*

SHOPPING

Madurai is famous for its cotton fabrics. Especially reasonable are the cotton saris, which are sold here in an unbelievable range of colours and patterns.

PUDUMANDAPAM MARKET ●

In the covered bazaar opposite the eastern entrance to the Meenakshi Temple, there are stalls selling lovely souvenirs such as books, essential oils, cushion covers and shawls. Around INSIDER TIP 250 skilled tailors will guarantee completion

Washing amid the aquatic plants – it's just routine for locals in Chettinad

of your made-to-measure garment within one hour. The best thing to do is order before your temple visit and collect the finished article afterwards. *Shop No. 126, Vijaya Stores*, turns out particularly good quality items very rapidly.

WHERE TO STAY

HOTEL CHENTOOR

One of the most popular budget hotels with 48 neatly furnished rooms, some with balcony, it is located just ten minutes away from the temple. There are great views from the ☀ rooftop *Emperor Restaurant. 106 West Perumal Maistry Street | tel. 0452 3 07 77 77 | www. hotelchentoor.in | Budget–Moderate*

THE GATEWAY HOTEL PASUMALAI MADURAI ☀

Housed in a colonial building more than a century old, this hotel has 63 rooms. Situated on a hill 3km (2mi) outside the city and surrounded by extensive grounds, it offers superb panoramic views of the temple city and the Kodai Hills. In addition, it boasts an open-air pool and an

Ayurveda and fitness centre. *40 TPK Rd | tel. 0452 2 37 16 01 | www.thegateway hotels.com | Moderate–Expensive*

GRT REGENCY

This modest business hotel is centrally located, very clean, has 55 functional rooms, a glass external lift and a fine restaurant with good cuisine. *38 Madakulam Rd | tel. 0452 2 37 11 55 | www.grtregency.com | Moderate*

INFORMATION

TOURIST INFORMATION

180 West Veli Street | more counters at the airport and train station | tel. 0452 2 33 47 57

WHERE TO GO

CHETTINAD (147 D–E4) (𝄞 F–G11)

In fact, this area comprises a collection of 74 villages, located between 80km (50mi) and 130km (81m) east of Madurai. Relatively little visited, it is still considered as something of an insider tip. Within this small area, there is an astonishing concentration of palatial houses and mansions, built in the 19th century by wealthy local bankers and businessmen. On account of its numerous different influences, the famed Chettinad cuisine is regarded as the most aromatic and refined in all India. Craftsmen working in the pretty villages still create authentic handicrafts. In the region's largest town, *Karaikudi* (pop. 86,000), it is possible to visit a sari weaving centre, and in *Athangudi* you can watch the production of wonderful tiles at *Sri Ganapathy Tiles (A. Muthuppattinam, Karaikudi Main Rd | tel. 04565 28 13 53)*. Many of the mansions can be visited. Some of them have evolved into beautiful hotels, such as the *Visalam (tel. 04565 27 33 01 | www.cghearth.com | Expensive)* in Kanadukathan/Karaikudi with 15 rooms, each over 1000 sq. ft., and a pool. The chef Pandiyamma spoils guests with her Chettinad specialities. Not far from here, the *Chettinadu Palace (daily 9am– 6pm | free admission | 11 AR Street, Kanadukathan)* is famous for its teak columns and antiques. Functional, practical and reasonably priced, the *Udhayam* hotel, centrally located at the Sivagangai bus stop in Karaikudi *(333 Sekkala Rd, Five Lamps | tel. 04565 22 33 23 | Budget)*, has 86 en-suite rooms.

KANYAKUMARI (CAPE COMORIN)
(146 C6) (*ETA* E13)

At the southernmost point of the subcontinent, where the Arabian Sea meets the Indian Ocean, lies Cape Comorin (pop. 23,000), a town known for its spectacular sunrises and sunsets. The entire area is also an important pilgrimage destination. Here, in 1948, a temple to Mahatma Gandhi was erected, the *Gandhi Mandapam*. And on the exact day of Gandhi's birthday, 2 October, the sun's rays fall on the spot where the urn containing the Mahatma's ashes was kept

for public viewing before immersion. On a rocky island, 500m offshore, the spiritual leader and philosopher Swami Vivekananda meditated uninterrupted from 25 to 27 December 1892. A boat *(daily 9am–4pm | Rs 30)* will take you out there to see the memorial to the swami, as well as to another small island where an enormous statue of the poet Thiruvalluvar (c. 200BC) stands.

Also right in the south, the beautiful, almost deserted sandy bay of INSIDER TIP *Vattakotai Beach*, 6km (4mi) northeast of Kanyakumari, is still a real hidden gem with its calm water and dense palm grove. There is a lovely view over the sickle-shaped bay from the 18th century *Vattakottai Fort*. The peaceful *Vivekananda Kendra Rest House (100 rooms | Vivekanandapuram | tel. 04652 27 12 50 | www.vkendra.org/accommodations | Budget)* has a large garden and free shuttle bus service to the town 2km away. *242km (150mi) southwest*

RAMESHWARAM BEACH
(147 E5) (*ETA* G12)

The sacred island of Rameshwaram with the temples of *Ramalingeshwaram, Gandhamandana Parvatam* and *Nambunayagi Amman Kali*, is located 163km (101mi) southeast of Madurai. It can be reached via a bridge from the mainland Its gently shelving beaches are lined with palm trees and are deserted, apart from local fishermen. The shallow, clear water is perfect for swimming and snorkelling.

THANJAVUR (TANJORE)
(147 E3) (*ETA* G10)

Situated in the fertile Kaveri Delta, the former capital of the Chola Empire (pop. 223,000)is now surrounded by rice paddies. Even today it boasts up to 90 temples. Among the most impressive is the 10th-century *Brihadeeswarar Temple daily 6am–1pm and 3–8pm),* a Unesco World Heritage Site. Constructed of red sandstone, the *gopuram* is an astonishing 72m (236ft) high, and the Nandi Bull is almost 6m (20ft) long and weighs 25 tons. The *Saraswati Mahal Library (Tue–Thu 10am–1pm and 1.30–5.30pm | Palace Campus | www.sarasvatimahallibrary.tn.nic.in),* which was installed in the *Thanjavur Palace* around 1700, is considered the most important historic library of the subcontinent. In addition to oriental and European works by poets and rulers, it contains more than 44,000 palm leaves inscribed with medical prescriptions and diagnoses in Sanskrit and Old Tamil. Behind the mighty walls of the Thanjavur Palace, which dates from around 1550 *(daily 9am–6pm | admission free | art gallery in the palace Rs 20),* impressive frescoes, an underground tunnel and the splendid *Durbar Hall,* the former reception hall of the king, feature amongst the highlights.

For accommodation in the city, try the *Parisutham (55-G A Canal Rd | tel. 04362 23 18 44 | www.hotelparisutham.com | Expensive).* With a location next to the canal, this modern hotel is laid out on terraces, has a lovely outdoor pool, an Ayurveda centre and 55 tastefully furnished rooms. Just 1km outside Thanjavur and beside a stream that flows between rice fields, the new *Paradise Resort (3/1216 Tanjore Main Rd, Darasuram, Ammapet, Kumabakonam | tel. 0435 2 41 64 69 | www.paradiseresortindia.com | Moderate)* consists of small bungalows with a total of 18 rooms, all furnished with antiques from the surrounding villages. The restaurant is in the 200-year-old main building, but you can also dine in tree houses. Such a peaceful location is perfect for an Ayurveda cure. Information: *Hotel Tamil Nadu Complex, Gandhiji Rd | tel. 04362 23 14 21. 158km (98mi) northeast*

TIRUCHIRAPPALLI (TRICHY)
(147 E3) *(ΩΩ G11)*

Situated to the north of Madurai, this green city (pop. 1,022,000) lies on the

Nothing to be scared of: the Brihadeeswarar Temple's very own elephant

Kaveri River. Towering on a rocky outcrop 5km (3mi) outside the town, the 83-m (272-ft) high ★ ⚒ *Rock Fort* is crowned by the *Ucchi Pillayar Temple (daily 6am–*

Shoulder ride in the temple city of Srirangam

8pm | video Rs 50). The rocks are said to be approx. 3.8 billion years old. Climbing to the fortress takes you up 344 steps; on the way are small cave temples dating from the 7th century. But the view is worth all the effort.

Some 6km (4mi) north of Tiruchirappalli, the legendary temple city of *Srirangam* is spread across a 1-sq. mi. island that is surrounded by two rivers – the Kaveri and the Kollidam. The *Sri Ranganathaswamy Temple (daily 6.15am–1pm and 3.15–8.45pm | camera Rs 20, video Rs 70 | tower ascent Rs 10)* dates from between the 14th and 17th century and with its 21 *gopuram*, is one of the largest in India. Dedicated to the Lord Vishnu it is an important centre of pilgrimage. It also boasts seven courtyards and an imposing 1000-columned hall. Adjacent, the *Jambukeshwara Temple (daily 6am–1pm and 4–9.30pm | camera Rs 20, video Rs 150)* is just as old though considerably smaller with only seven *gopuram*. Remember that non-Hindus are not allowed in the holy of holies. The temple is built around a *Shiva lingam* that stands in a sacred spring.

Around 3km (2mi) from the centre, the *Ashby Hotel (17 A Junction Rd | tel. 0431 2 46 06 52 | www.ashbyhotel.com | Budget)* exudes nostalgia. The furnishings in this merchant's house dating from 1923 are made of teak, and ceiling fans whir in all 20 rooms. Prices at the 4-star hotel *Sangam (Collector's Office Rd | tel. 0431 2 41 47 00 | www.hotelsangam.com | Expensive)* are higher, but then it has a health club and pool among its facilities. Information: *Tourist Information Centre, Williams Rd | tel. 0431 2 46 01 36*. 95km (59mi) north

UDHAGAMAN-DALAM (OOT-ACAMUND OR OOTY)

(146 B2) *(ⓜ D10)* ★ **Between 1858 and 1947, to escape from the summer**

...eat of the plains, the British Raj with-
...rew to the cooler climes of the hills.
...rom there, they even managed to carry
...n with government business, and thus
...he so-called *hill stations* such as *Ooty,
Munnar, Coonoor* and *Kodaikanal* became very well known in South India.
...he temperature in the highlands can dip
...s low as freezing in the winter.

...lestled in a hilly landscape, amongst
...green tea plantations and forests of pine
...and eucalyptus, the 'Queen of the Hill
...tations', as Ooty (pop. 233,000) was
...nown, was established in the early 19th
...entury. It extends across broad slopes,
...ts pretty cottages with their flowerbeds
...ordering the winding roads. On the pe-
...iphery, however, the more blighted ar-
...as resemble Brazilian slums.

...he British would spend their time in
...Ooty playing tennis and golf, riding and
...ocialising. Today it's more about trek-
...king. With its recreational activities, the
...hill resort is still a very relaxing place to
...be.

SIGHTSEEING

BOTANICAL GARDEN

With its large areas of lawn, this park-like
garden covering 50 acres was created by
the British in 1847. It gently rolls across
the hillside and has a very English feel.
Standing alongside the rare trees, shrubs
and flowers, there is also a 20 million-
year-old fossilised tree trunk. In the eastern part, on the *toda mund* (hill), you
can visit the small, Toda tribe settlement.
*Daily 8am–6.30pm | Rs 20, camera Rs 30,
video Rs 300*

ST STEPHEN'S CHURCH

This cream-coloured Gothic structure dates
back to 1820. It is said that the wood for
the construction was taken by British soldiers from Tipu Sultan's Palace in Sriranga-
patnam and brought to Ooty by elephant.
The most distinctive feature of the church
is the *Clock Tower. Mysore Rd*

THE THREAD GARDEN

Fifty women worked on this project for 12
years, using up almost 60 million metres
of thread, and ultimately creating an artificial embroidery garden of colourful
flowers, plants, lotus ponds, etc. This
four-dimensional embroidery is a new
technique, done without any machines
or needles, entirely by hand. *On North
Lake Rd opposite the boathouse | Rs 10 |
www.threadgarden.com*

FOOD & DRINK

DHABA EXPRESS

A simple restaurant which serves good
North Indian food. *Lake view, opposite
the boathouse | tel. 0423 2 44 46 33 |
Budget*

GARDEN CAFÉ

This coffee shop opens out into a garden
and offers typical South Indian snacks
such as *idli* and *dosa. Nahar Nilgiris,
Charing Cross | Budget*

SIDE WALK CAFÉ

Italy meets India, namely in the form of
pizza and cappuccino, enriched with
American burgers and sandwiches. Nice
design and good service. *Commercial Rd |
Budget*

SHOPPING

TIBETAN MARKET

Tibetan refugees sell woolly hats, scarves,
gloves and slippers. They also have colourful *tankas,* wall hangings with spiritual symbols. *Opposite the entrance to the
Botanical Garden*

UDHAGAMANDALAM (OOTY)

BOATS

At the boathouse on the artificially created lake there are all kinds of craft for hire. *6am until sunset | Rs 75 for 30 min for a pedalo, Rs 300 for 20 min for a motorboat*

RIDING

It's fun to take a ride along the soft trails outside town. Beginners have a guide to lead the horses. They are usually at places where tourists gather. *From approx. Rs 100 for 30 min*

TREKKING

The *Dodabetta–Snowdon–Ooty Walk* begins at the *Dodabetta Junction.* An easy path winds down through the forest to Ooty. It takes three to four hours and is not tiring. In contrast the two-day tour, *Ooty–Avalanche–Upper Bhavani–Kolaribetta–Emerald–Ooty,* requires a certain level of fitness. *It leads from* Ooty 24km (15mi) southwest to the Avalanche Dam. After a night spent in the *Forest Department Guest House (Wildlife Office Ooty)* you continue the next day to the Upper Bhavani Lake. A short stretch passes through the *Mukurthi National Park* to Mt Kolaribetta. The climb to the 2625-m (8612-ft) summit is not very taxing and the views are magnificent. On the way back, heading in a northeasterly direction, you will pass the Emerald Lake from where there are buses back to Ooty. Information: *Office Wildlife Warden, starts on Church Hill Rd | tel. 0423 2 44 40 98*

Just how popular the ● movies are in India is demonstrated by the number of cinemas (seven) to be found in Ooty alone. Even if the Bollywood movie isn't dubbed into English, treat yourself to the experience and see how the audience laughs, cries and loves with the actors. Great theatre at the cinema.

Not typically Indian, but nice for a change: pedalos on the lake in Ooty

WHERE TO STAY

AAKRITI

This boutique-style eco-homestay lies 19km (12mi) outside Ooty among the tea plantations. It has two very comfortably furnished cottages, and guests eat together with the young Viswakumar family. There are cooking classes which also include farm visits (Rs 1500, cooking classes free if you stay more than three nights). The hosts are happy to take guests on excursions to sights in the vicinity. *399 Coonoor Rd, Coonoor | tel. 094 43 85 19 35 | www.eco homestay.com | Moderate–Expensive*

FERNHILL PALACE

Live like a sahib or memsahib in the colonial period – the former summer residence of the Maharajas of Mysore, with its 30 suites including jacuzzi, conveys precisely this feeling. In the evening, guests gather around the fireplace, in the morning they are woken up with a cup of tea. *Fernhill Post | tel. 0423 2 44 39 10 | www. welcomheritagehotels.com | Expensive*

THE NILGIRI WOODLANDS

This old colonial building with its teak furniture and open fireplaces has 29 rooms, each one individually furnished and decorated. In front runs a communal veranda with a view of the racecourse. *Race Course Rd | tel. 0423 2 44 25 51 | Moderate*

INFORMATION

TOURIST INFORMATION

Wenlock Rd | tel. 0423 2 44 39 77

WHERE TO GO

DODDABETTA ☆ (146 B2) *(ひ D10)*

At an altitude of 2638m (8655ft) this is the highest point in the Niligiris and its viewing tower offers fantastic views of the surrounding area. Doddabetta means 'high mountain' and it lies some 10km (6mi) east of Ooty, on the border between the Eastern and Western Ghats. You can get to the summit by bus.

MUDUMALAI WILDLIFE SANCTUARY (146 A–B2) *(ひ D–E10)*

Covering an area of 124 sq. mi., this large nature reserve forms part of the *Jawaharlal Nehru National Park*. Located 36km (22mi) northwest of Oot, it was the first wildlife sanctuary in India *and it provides* a wide variety of landscapes – lowlands, open steppe, swamps and valleys. Elephants, tigers, panthers, red deer and macaque monkeys are all native to the area. Elephant rides and minibus tours are available. *Admission Rs 35* From bamboo huts to luxury resorts or tree-houses, every nature lover will find suitable accommodation in the *Jungle Retreat (Bokkapuram, Masinagudi | tel. 0423 2526469 | www.jungleretreat.com | Budget)*. Away from civilisation, no TV or telephone, but in the national park.

INSIDER TIP ▶ PYKARA (146 B2) *(ひ E10)*

Pykara has for centuries been the homeland of the *Toda*, one of the last remaining mountain tribes of this region. They live in barrel-shaped huts made of grass and bamboo. These buffalo herders are happy to show you their settlements, known as *sholas*.
On the way there, it's worth stopping at the ☆ boathouse by the dam on the Pykara River to enjoy the beautiful view. *21km (13mi) northeast*

TRIBAL RESEARCH CENTER (146 B2) *(ひ E10)*

Displays both inside and outside the museum offer insights into the culture of the different hill tribes, especially the *Toda (Mon–Fri 10am–5pm | admission free). 11 km (7 miles) southeast*

TRIPS & TOURS

The tours are marked in green in the road atlas,
pull-out map and on the back cover

1 A FUN RIDE: THE STEAM TRAIN TO OOTY ✻

Since 2005 the Blue Mountain Railway has been one of the 'Mountain Railways of India', a Unesco World Heritage Site shared by the Darjeeling Himalayan Railway and the Kalka Shimla Railway. It winds its way through the Nilgiri Hills from Mettupalayam up to Udhagamandalam (Ooty) along a metre-gauge track that employs a rack and pinion system for the steep sections. Work on this British engineering marvel began in 1891 and was completed in 1908. Along the 46-km (29-mi) route the little train climbs almost ust under 5 hours.

At the very latest, by the time passengers reach the fourth of the twelve stations, they will have got to know how things work aboard the Toy Train, as the INSIDER TIP▶ Blue Mountain Railway (Nilgiri = 'Blue Mountain') is otherwise known. The tiny stations look as if they've been plucked straight out of some neatly laid out toy railway. At each one, travellers jump out of their compartments and run across the tracks to fetch tea and snacks from vendors, plus garlands of flowers to wear. Everyone chats, shares food and changes places according to the view. And how spectacular that is. In a huge cloud of steam, the locomotive chugs into the hills, travels across 26, in part impossibly narrow bridges and viaducts, and over yawning chasms, such as the one at the steepest

Photo: Munnar, tea plantations overlooking Mattupetty Lake

Heading for the mountains, you can climb up under your own steam or hop aboard a picture-book train

section of the **Hulikal Gorge**. It hisses through dense jungle and green tea plantations. Occasionally, elephants will trot alongside for a short distance, monkeys often crouch in the trees and on rooftops, while as passengers lean out as far as they can and wave back at every bend in the track. When it's going really slowly, children will jump on the running board and peer curiously into the compartments, with just an ignoring wink from the conductor. The train passes through a total of 16 tunnels. Engine driv-

ers allow some passengers to join them in the open cab, which is decorated with flowers and pictures. But the heat is almost unbearable and soot quickly blackens the face.

The rack and pinion section finishes in **Coonoor**, where a diesel locomotive takes over. When you start to smell the eucalyptus, you'll know you've almost arrived in **Ooty** → p. 110. And among those waiting on the platform will be – a cow … and a man brushing his teeth seemingly unperturbed by the usual pan-

All aboard the 'Toy Train'

and fauna, is a very special experience. This two-day trip with a knowledgeable guide to the top of Meesappulimala will take you among mountain goats and elephants, colourful butterflies and violet rhododendrons to a height of 2640m (8661ft), with two overnight stays in tent camps.

Located 25km (16mi) east of Munnar → p. 57. Meesappulimala is the second-highest summit in the region. To go trekking on the mountain you first need to get a permit from the *Kerala Forest Development Corporation office (KFDC)*. It's possible to go on a guided walk, with guide/porters who will carry your pack, cook and explain the flora and fauna on the way.

After an induction by a naturalist at the Silent Valley Estate, the group leaves Munnar and climbs for around three hours up to the Land's End Camp at a height of 2325m (7627ft). The trail leads through high-altitude tea, coffee and cardamom plantations. Tall ferns in the vast meadows of the Shola Grasslands provide shelter for deer, bison and giant squirrels. Flower lovers will delight in the sight of wild orchids speckling the meadows. The evergreen rainforests and grassy hills also provide habitat and protection for the endangered *Nilgiri tahr,* a native species of brown-coloured mountain goat. Although the animals glance curiously at hikers from the slopes, they are too shy to come any closer.

Just in time for the sunset, the guide will lead the group to a particularly good ☼ viewpoint. From there you can appreciate the startling contrast between the deep shadow cast by Mt Anamudi on the other mountain slopes, and the red glow bathing its summit. At 2695m (8842ft), this is the highest mountain in the Western Ghats and indeed the whole of South India. Nobody utters a word;

demonium you get at Indian stations, airports and bus stations, amid shouts of 'taxi? hotel? porter?' From Ooty you can either return to Mettupalayam the way you came or take the bus to Bengaluru, Calicut, Kanyakumari, Kochi, Mysore, Thanjavur and Tirupathi. Blue Mountain Railway: *departs Mettupalayam daily 7.10am, arrives Ooty at midday | tickets at the station | Ooty Rd | tel. 04254 22 22 85 | advance booking online at www.indianrail.in, the codes for Mettupalayam and Ooty are MTP and UAM, train No. 56136 | one-way 2nd-class ticket including booking fee Rs 33; 1st class (thoroughly recommended for the views) Rs 150.*

2 HIKING TO THE TOP OF MEESAPPULIMALA

 Hiking in the magnificent scenery of the Western Ghats, with their huge variety of flora the symphony of birdsong that fills the air at this time provides background music that cannot be bettered.

The first night is spent at the **Land's End Camp**, in two-man tents; mats and sleeping bags are provided. In the surrounding eucalyptus and pine forests, the resident birds will make sure you wake up in good time in the morning. It takes about two hours to get to the ☀ summit. The 360-degree view of the tea plantations far below, the twinkling blue lakes and, with good visibility, the hill tops of Kodaikanal, another hill station, is simply overwhelming. After a decent rest, the descent follows one of the numerous mountain tracks down to the second night's accommodation, the **Rhodo Valley Camp** at 2325m (7627ft). The name says it all: it lies in the heart of a wild rhododendron grove. Another trail leads past **Anaerangal Lake**, where with a bit of luck you'll see elephants quenching their thirst. Not far from here is the **Papathy Shol**, the butterfly forest. In October/November especially, thousands of colourful butterflies in myriad colours and patterns swirl through the sparse mixed forest producing an almost surreal visual experience.

The two days, including guide, food, accommodation and collection from your accommodation in Munnar, cost around £55 per person, provided the booking is for a total of four people *(Marvel Tours Pvt. Ltd | Kochi | tel. 0484 2 33 54 44 | www.marveltours.in)*. Trekking specialist *Muddy Boots* offers a similar deal *(tel. 095 44 20 12 49 | www.muddyboots.in)*. For individual trekking contact *Kerala Forest Development Corporation, KFDC Office | Aaranyakom, Karapuzha, Kootayam | tel. 0481 2 58 26 40* or *District Tourist Promotion Council Office | Munnar | tel. 04865 23 15 16*

3 IN THE TIGER RESERVE WITH SMUGGLERS AND POACHERS

🚶 INSIDER TIP **Nature watching with former smugglers and poachers** – it doesn't get more authentic than that. As part of an eco-development project for the social inclusion of the hill tribes – set up a decade or so ago – these tough guys were trained as nature guides and now accompany groups on bamboo rafting and trekking tours through the virgin Periyar Tiger Reserve in Kerala's Western Ghats.

Thankkappan admits to having killed 36 elephants but now adds 'unfortunately' - as that was in his past life as a poacher. Today he's still carrying a gun, but it's just

Nilgiri tahr – very shy and very endangered

Trekkers can relax as the guide paddles the bamboo raft across the Periyar reservoir

to protect the trekking group from tigers, leopards, wild elephants and bears. Ravi Thavan, another guide, belongs to the 600-family Mannan, one of three mountain tribes living around Thekkady who have managed to preserve their identity to the present day. Ravi did not go to school; he learned his passable English from tourists. Formerly a fisherman, he also collected wild honey and firewood, and smuggled sandalwood, teak and precious rosewood across the ridge separating Kerala from the neighbouring state of Tamil Nadu. Today, he has a part-time job on night patrol in the forests, ambushing his old smuggling colleagues. It isn't just the five guides in the ten-person group (maximum number of members), plus the armed security guard, that make this trek so different; just walking in the jungle itself, through the densest part of the Periyar National Park, is something very special.

On the evening before departure, a naturalist gives the group an introduction to the flora and fauna at the *Spice Village* hotel in Thekaddy, but remember: don't expect any luxury, just a wilderness adventure. The walk begins at 8am about 2km away, on the shore of the 10-sq. mi. Periyar Reservoir. Members are given knee-high gaiters that protect against wet and nasty pond life and creepy-crawlies.

One by one, the bamboo rafts are pulled by rope across the narrow channel to where, on the opposite bank, the trekking tour begins. The guides stop repeatedly to explain the medical uses of certain plants and point out bird songs. It's no easy job; after all, there are 322 different species living here. The Periyar

Animal Sanctuary and **Tiger Reserve** cover an area of around 350 sq. mi., of which a 130-sq. mi. chunk of the central zone has been declared a national park and is not accessible to visitors. However, tourists can explore within a buffer zone of 21 sq. mi. around the lake. More than 74 percent of the area consists of evergreen tropical plants, forest and grassland; 145 different species of orchid alone thrive in this, one of the most diverse national parks in India.

In single file, the group walks through man-high elephant grass and evergreen rainforests of bamboo shrubs and tropical trees. The Malabar giant squirrel climbs up the trunks, a Nilgiri langur gorges itself on the crimson fruit of the flowering murdah. *Gaur*, a species of bison, wild dogs and even scorpions might cross the path, but thanks to the sturdy gaiters there's no danger of being bitten. Elephant dung on the path will indicate to the guides the trail of the gentle giants. With a bit of luck, you'll encounter a magnificent bull with great curved tusks, accompanied by his harem. Just in case, guides like Thankkappan carefully draw their guns and get in position, but the elephants usually show no interest whatsoever in the excited pack of people, and continue nonchalantly on their way. Of course, every group will hope to also spot a tiger. However, it isn't very likely, because there are only about 30 specimens living in the entire reserve. Fresh paw prints and scratches on trees testify to their presence. According to the guides, the tigers scrape their claws on the trunk because the sap makes them even sharper.

Tea is taken in a **tent camp**. The small hill is completely surrounded by a ditch, which during the two-day photo safari keeps uninvited guests at bay.

On the next stage, the rafts are deployed again. They have space for a maximum of four members and two guides, who steer and paddle the bamboo raft using long poles. White ibis perch on the numerous broken tree trunks sticking out of the water. Herons and cormorants glide over the bamboo armada. Periyar provides a habitat for 322 species of bird, of which a third are winter migrants, remaining here from September to the end of March. From the shore, you can see the main ridge of the Western Ghats, the mountains that form the border between Kerala and Tamil Nadu, with the 2019-m (6624-ft) high Mount Kottamala being the highest summit in this area.

Before departure, the guides hold a small ceremony for the goddess of the forest, Vandevi. If she's appeased, the conditions will be calm and the men won't have to struggle too much, paddling the rafts. But they're also happy to let members have a go at paddling. Rafting – trekking – rafting – trekking – that's how the tour is planned. Afterwards, the team rustles up a beautiful meal, which is eaten under shady trees. The guides will also tell you about their lives as smugglers and poachers, which, while it would have earned them more money than they receive now, was also much more dangerous. However, they regain some of that lost excitement with their night-time smuggler hunting forays.

Information in Thekkady: *Periyar Tiger Reserve Organisation | Lake Rd | tel. 04869 22 20 27 or Forest Information and Reservation Centre | Ambady Junction, Lake Rd | tel. 04869 32 20 28 | both daily 6am–7pm or at the Spice Village Hotel | Kumily Rd | tel. 04869 22 45 14 | www. cghearth.com. Periyar National Park opening times 7am–5pm | admission Rs 300 | whole-day trekking with bamboo rafting Rs 1500, with one night in the tent camp Rs 4000, 2 nights Rs 6000*

SPORTS & ACTIVITIES

Most visitors to South India come for the swimming or sightseeing; many combine the two. Seasoned travellers, however, know that the hills and the sea hold so many different opportunities for active holidaymakers.

And if you want to impress people with South Indian specialities when you get home, simply join a local cooking class.

BOLLYWOOD DANCING

Bollywood films with their amazing dance routines are not only popular in South India. Movie choreographer Arun Kumar teaches novices in Bengaluru the INSIDER TIP Bollywood dance moves. *Studio 1: Alliance Française | 108 Thimmaiah Rd, Vasanthnagar; Studio 2:*

Bangalore School of Music | 8 HMT/HBCS/ CBI Rd, RT Nagar | tel. 095 35 00 74 69 | Rs 350 for an hour's one-to-one tuition | www.zealers.com

COOKING

Learning Indian cooking in the country itself, with fresh ingredients and local spices, is a very special experience. Such courses are mainly offered by hotels and restaurants. You will learn about preparing fresh fish and seafood, as well as Kerala's varied vegetarian repertoire in cooking classes run by *Bhakti Kutir (296, Colomb,Palolem, Goa | tel. 0832 2 64 34 69 | www.bhaktikutir.com)*. In Calangute, Ambica Coelho gives demonstrations at the *O'Pescador restaurant*

Cricket, cooking or yoga: activities for outdoor enthusiasts, keen cooks and those who like mental and physical exercise

(Baga Rd, Cobra Vaddo | tel. 0832 2 27 94 47). In Kanadukathan, Paniyamma familiarises visitors with the much-praised INSIDER TIP *Chettinad* cuisine *(Hotel Visalam | tel. 04565 27 33 01 | www.cghearth.com)*. Authentic Kerala cuisine is prepared at the *Coconut Palms Heritage Resort* in Alleppey *(tel. 0471 2 33 04 17)*.

For those who don't have much time, chef Branca gives two-hour classes in Goan cuisine for around £20 *(José Falcao Rd, Panaji | tel. 098 22 13 18 35)*. Similarly in Kochi, Nimmy Paul will teach you how to prepare wonderful Kerala cuisine in two-hour cooking classes *(Chakkalakkal Rd, Varaimparambil | approx. Rs 1600 | tel. 0484 2 31 42 93 | www.nimmypaul. com)*.

CRICKET

Nowhere is more passionate about cricket than India. Almost the entire nation defines itself through this sport, which the British introduced to the subcontinent in around 1900. Visit one of the large stadiums to experience the special atmosphere of a game at first-hand. *The M. A. Chidambaram Stadium Chennai (Wallajah Rd | tel. 044 28514896 | 50,000 spectators)* occupies a special place in Indian cricketing history: in 1962 it was the venue for the country's first win over England. The *M. Chinnaswamy Stadium Bangalore (Cubbon Rd/Queens Rd | tel. 080 40154015)* can accommodate up to 55,000 spectators. The *Goa Cricket Team* is based at the *Dr Rajendra Prasad Stadium Margao (Quepem Rd | tel. 0832 2731495)*. Tickets cost anything between Rs 160 and Rs 12,000.

DIVING & SNORKELLING

South India's best dive sites are located in the north of Karnataka, off *Pigeon Island* opposite Bhatkal. An impressive underwater world opens up among the reefs and numerous wrecks. In Goa most dive boats head for *San Jorge Island* or *Grande Island*. Wrecks of Spanish and Portuguese galleons lie on the seabed, as well as a ship from World War II. Dive centres: *Goa Diving | No. 145-P Chapel Bhat, Chicalim | tel. 0832 555117; Barracuda Diving | c/o Cidade de Goa Beach Resort, Dona Paula; Dreamz Diving | tel. 097 40752480 | www.dreamzdiving. com.* The *PADI Diving Centre* on the beach between the *Lutz Hotel* and *Hotel Daphne (tel. 044 27443115 | www.tem pleadventures.com)* offers a diving tour to the legendary seven sunken temples off Mamallapuram. Further information at: *www.padi.com*

GOLF

Many old clubhouses still have lots of colonial charm, such as the *Bangalore Golf Club* dating from 1876 *(18-hole | 2 Sankey Rd, High Grounds | tel. 080 4348 4949)* or the *Madras Gymkhana Club* in Chennai *(18-hole | Anna Salai | tel. 044 25368160 | www.madrasgymkhana. com)*. The *Ootacamund Gymkhana Club* dates from 1896; its course lies on steep terrain at an altitude of 2300m/7600ft *(18-hole | Ekaly Rd | tel. 0423 2442254 | www.ootygolfclub.org)*.

MOTORBIKE TOURS

Riding a motorbike in India is certainly not without its dangers. Traffic is often hazardous and you need time to get used to the rhythm, particularly in the cities. You can hire bikes and scooters everywhere. There are also specialist operators: Vintage Rides based in Delhi offers Royal Enfield motorcycle tours to enthusiasts in most parts of the country including Goa, Kerala and Karnataka (tel. 091 11 41 00 78 06 | *www.vintagerides. com)*. *Enfield Point*, who operate out of Manali, also offer a dedicated Bullet tour of South India *(tel. 091 98 05 28 47 64 | www.enfieldpoint.com)*. *There are also a number of operators based in the UK.*

TREKKING

The Western Ghats, which include the Nilgiri Mountains, are a great place for trekking. Rising to a maximum altitude of approx. 2600m (8500ft), these mountains are easily accessible for every hiker. For trails that are hard to follow and lead through jungle areas, trekkers should acquire a guide from the respective Forest Department. To traverse protected areas you will also need to have a permit. Nilgiri Mountains: *Wildlife Warden | Mahalingam Buildings, Coonoor Rd, Udhagamandalam | tel. 0423 2444098;* Munnar: *Forest Information Centre | tel. 04865 231587;* Kumily: *Department of*

Tourism | Thekkady Jn | tel. 04869 32 26 20. Organised walks are operated by the *District Tourism Promotion Council (DTPC) | Old Munnar | tel. 0045 23 15 16.* Further information from *Muddy Boots*, experts in trekking and mountain-biking

There are two reputable centres located in Bengaluru: *Institute of Naturopathy & Yogic Sciences (INYS) | Tumkur Rd, Jindal Nagar | tel. 080 23 71 77 77 | www.jindal naturecure.org* and *Svyasa Yoga University | 19 Eknath Bhavan, Gavipuram Circle,*

As well as colourful reefs and fish, sunken wrecks await divers

tours, as well as contact point for general questions on trekking in South India *(in England – Pradeep Murthy – tel. 0044 78 26 72 87 07, in India 095 44 20 12 49 | www.muddyboots.in).* The best times for trekking are April to June and September to December.

YOGA

Many hotels and resorts offer yoga classes. The morning group sessions are mostly free. There's a big choice of yoga centres and courses in INSIDER TIP *Auroville*. The inexpensive accommodation there may enable visitors to attend courses for longer *(tel. 0413 2 62 27 04 | www.auroville.org).*

K. G. Nagar | tel. 080 26 60 86 45 | www. svyasa.org. At the *Ashtanga Yoga Research Institute* in Mysore they teach rapid breathing exercises *(2358th Cross, Gokulam | tel. 098 80 18 55 00 | www. kpjayi.org)*, while at the *Krishnamacharya Yoga Mandiram* in Chennai they do viniyoga, a gentler version of yoga *(31 Fourth Cross Street, R K Nagar | tel. 044 24 93 79 98 | www.kym.org).* Also in Chennai, in the early morning from 6–8am you can join in ● free yoga classes at a total of 26 public open spaces, including Panagal Park and Marina Beach. With the health of his fellow citizens at heart, Chennai's former mayor had the necessary stages built and appointed yoga instructors.

TRAVEL WITH KIDS

What sounds like an advertising slogan for the tourism sector is, in fact, the case: Indians love children. And that isn't just a good thing for the kids but also for the grown-ups, as children often help everyone make friends. South India is tremendously exciting territory for the young. The exotic animals, the giant sand pit known as the beach, and all the friendly people, who never complain when things get a bit noisy and boisterous. But there are a few things you should consider if you're travelling with children in South India. One is of course the strong tropical sun, which will necessitate a sun hat and using sunscreen with a very high protection factor. Then there is the hot and spicy food, which youngsters probably won't be used to; always ask for milder dishes for the kids. And finally there are all those dogs - they might look nice and playful, but be careful, they can also bite!

GOA

ANCESTRAL GOA (140 A5) (*ⓓ B6*)
At the so-called *Big Foot Village* in Loutolim (9km/6mi from Margao, 45km/28mi from Calangute), colourful, naive figures and props give children a fun introduction to the roots of Goan culture. *Daily 9am–6pm | admission Rs 50 | www.ancestralgoa.com*

DONA SYLVIA BEACH RESORT (140 A5) (*ⓓ B6*)
This pretty resort in Cavelossim has the feel of holiday centre. It offers a daily programme for children, with a kids' club, playground, pool, numerous games and competitions. Supervisors are available who will look after the little ones when their parents want to do something else. *Tel. 0832 2 871 88 | www.donasylvia. com | Expensive*

KERALA

WONDERLA KOCHI (146 A4) (*ⓓ D11*)
A large theme park with water slides, rides, musical fountains and many other attractions. It has a sister company in Bangalore. *Mon–Fri 10.30am–6pm, Sat/ Sun 10.30am–7pm | admission adults from Rs 520, children from Rs 420 | Pallikara near Kakkanad, 14km (9mi) northeast of Kochi | www.wonderla.com*

Indians love children: youngsters will find plenty of exciting things to do, from riding on an elephant to visiting a crocodile farm

KARNATAKA

PILIKULA BIOLOGICAL PARK (143 E4) (∅ C9)
Children can go riding on elephants at the Pilikula Biological Park near Mangalore. There are also lots of other animals to look at, as well as a funfair with giant slide, a water park and boating lake. *Wed–Mon 11am–1pm and 4–6pm | admission from 15 yrs and over Rs 50, under 15 Rs 20 | Moodushedde, Vamanjoor | www.pilikula.com*

TAMIL NADU

CROCODILE PARK (145 F4) (∅ H9)
South of Chennai, various species of Indian crocodiles as well as alligators live in open-air pools. *Tue–Sun 8.30am–5.30pm | admission Rs 35, children up to 10 Rs 10 | 42km/26mi from Chennai, on the coast road towards Mamallapuram | www.madrascrocodilebank.org*

GAME PARKS

South India has lots of game parks, notably in the state of Karnataka. The *Bandipur National Park* **(146 B1–2) (∅ D–E10)** in the borderlands of Kerala, Karnataka and Tamil Nadu, for example, is a designated tiger reserve. Near Coorg in Karnataka, the *Dubare Elephant Camp* **(143 F5) (∅ D9)** is home to 150 elephants. However, most of the region's wild Asian elephants live in the *Nagarhole National Park* **(144 A5) (∅ D9)**. Along with tigers and leopards, the pachyderms are also found in the *Bhadra Tiger Reserve* **(143 F3) (∅ C–D8)**. The *Mudumalai Wildlife Sanctuary* **(146 A–B2) (∅ D–E10)** covers an area of 124 sq. mi. and contains a large variety of animals, including elephants, panthers, bears, monkeys. You can find detailed information about animals and tours at *www.indianwildlifeportal.com, www.wild-india.com, www.indiawildliferesorts.com and www.indian-wildlife.com*.

FESTIVALS & EVENTS

1 January New Year's Day; **26 January** Republic Day; **1 May** *Labour Day*; **15 August** Independence Day; **2 October** Gandhi's Birthday; **25 December** Christmas

RELIGIOUS HOLIDAYS

Most religious holidays are calculated according to the lunar calendar and are therefore movable.

6 JANUARY

The festival of ▶ *Epiphany* is celebrated in Goa – principally in Cansaulim, Chandor and Reis Magos.

END FEBRUARY/BEGINNING MARCH

▶ ⭐ *Shivaratri* or *Mahashivaratri*: the Night of Shiva is the holiest night for Hindus and is spent at the temple.

MARCH

The Indian ▶ *Holi Festival* is celebrated especially colourfully in Goa, where it is known as the *Shigmo Festival*. Temple festivals, parades, processions.

AUGUST

▶ *Janmashtami:* Krishna's Birthday, involving midnight festivals at the Hindu temples.

SEPTEMBER/OCTOBER

▶ ⭐ *Dussehra:* India's best-known festival is celebrated in different ways in different places. It celebrates the victory of the gods Rama and Durga over the demons. In the South it is called *Navaratri.* In Tamil Nadu and Kerala the festivities go on for nine nights; in Mysore it lasts ten days and includes music festivals in the illuminated palace. On the tenth day an impressive procession of elephants leads to the Maharaja's palace.

NOVEMBER/DECEMBER

▶ INSIDER TIP ▶ *Divali* – the Festival of Light: everywhere fireworks illuminate the sky and small oil lamps are lit in honour of Lakshmi, the goddess of wealth and prosperity. She only visits those who show her the way with lights.

FESTIVALS

JANUARY

At the ▶ *Float Festival* in Madurai, temple deities are paraded around the sacred Mariamman Teppakolam Lake on a brightly decorated float.

▶ *Pongal* is the name given to the harvest festival, which takes place during the religious celebrations of *Makar Sank-*

Elephants on parade, snake boat races, festivals of light – South Indian celebrations are always full of pomp and splendour

ranti. Cows are decorated with balloons and garlands, and their horns colourfully painted before they are led through the streets to musical accompaniment.

FEBRUARY

This ▶ *Food & Cultural Festival* which lasts between three to five days is held alternately in Panaji and Margao; it includes cooking contests, stalls selling typical Goan food, and lots of music and dance.

FEBRUARY/MARCH

The ancient ▶ *Natyanjali Dance Festival* was revived 25 years ago at the Nataraja Temple in Chidambaram. Famous dancers from all over India come to this five-day festival in honour of Shiva as Nataraja, the 'Lord of Dance'; now, celebrations are held not only here but at many other temples in Tamil Nadu.

Carnival or ▶ *Mardi Gras* is celebrated all over Goa. On the first day, *Fat Saturday*, 'King Momo' leads a parade of competing, colourfully-dressed teams through the streets.

APRIL/MAY

During the eight-day ▶ *Pooram Festival* (summer harvest festival) at Thrissur in Kerala, various temples compete to see who has the most beautiful parade of finely decorated elephants. There are also Kathakali performances and firework displays.

AUGUST/SEPTEMBER

Kerala's snake boat races are linked with the ▶ *Onam,* the harvest festival. Each boat has a compliment of 25 singers and 125 rowers. The most famous regatta is the *Nehru Trophy* on Punnamada Lake in Alappuzha. It is also held during the tourist season in December/January.

MID-DECEMBER–MID-JANUARY

At the ▶ ● *Chennai Music and Dance Festival* artists from all over India play classical music and perform traditional dances on squares, at temples and in heritage bungalows. More than 2000 people take part in over 300 concerts.

LINKS, BLOGS, APPS & MORE

LINKS

▶ www.mapsofindia.com   One of the most valuable links for South India travellers. Here you will find detailed maps and train and flight connections, also for the rest of India

▶ www.keralatourism.org, www.goatourism.gov.in, www.karnatakatourism. org, www.tamilnadutourism.org These are the official tourism websites of the four states covered in this guide. They have detailed information about all the different aspects of the destination, the Kerala site, for example, having a comprehensive list of Ayurveda centres

▶ www.discoverbangalore.com Everything about India's Silicon Valley – Bangalore. This site has continuously updated information and tips on all kinds of themes related to the city: events, restaurants, sights and much more

▶ www.wwfindia.org and www.traffic.org Protecting wildlife means thinking about it before you buy a souvenir in South India. Especially if they're products made of crocodile skin, ivory, coral, or certain protected plants. WWF and Traffic India explain all the issues on their websites

BLOGS & FORUMS

▶ www.goablog.org Goa's top beaches, the best parties, the most effective yoga courses, its history, culture and politics, upcoming events – bloggers from around the world share interesting information on a large range of themes relating to India's smallest state

▶ paradise-kerala.com/blog Articles written by Sunu Philip and Ratheesh R. Nath covering a broad range of Kerala-related topics of interest to tourists, from 'Elephants and Kerala Culture' to cuisine to 'Offbeat Destinations'. Regular posts keep the site fresh and up to date. Includes some excellent photography

▶ www.expat-blog.com/en/destination/asia/india/ There are contingents

Regardless of whether you are still preparing your trip or already in India: these addresses will provide you with more information, videos and networks to make your holiday even more enjoyable.

of expatriate Brits, Americans and others dotted around India. Pictures, classified ads and a very lively forum. If you need specific information, then best to ask someone who lives there. This thread includes blogs from Bangalore, Chennai, Tamil Nadu and Karnataka

VIDEOS & STREAMS

▶ www.youtube.com Search for any topic you like from 'Kathakali' to 'Tamil music', 'Mamallapuram' to 'Munnar' and 'Goan beaches' to 'Kerala Backwaters' to get revealing footage of South India

▶ www.360cities.net The 360° panoramic photos give an all-round view of top sights. Check out the rotating views of the Mysore Palace, Sri Meenakshi Temple in Madurai at night, the Chinese fishing nets in Kochi and many more

APPS

▶ Indian Rail Info This free app provides arrival and departure information for trains, shows available seats/sleepers, ticket prices and much more

▶ Localbeat Besides business directory and restaurants, this app has information on topics ranging from Hollywood and Bollywood movies to theatre and events to the regional weather and news from the major dailies

NETWORKS

▶ www.couchsurfing.org The 'Couchsurfing' network puts travellers in touch with people in the countries and cities they are visiting

▶ short.travel/inds6 The Thorntree community swaps experiences and useful tips from all around the South Indian regions, cities and sites: the most reliable forms of transport to get to a given place, especially cheap accommodation, or restaurants that should be avoided . Simply enter 'Kerala', for example, at the end of the URL

▶ www.tripadvisor.co.uk/www.tripadvisor.com Online forum, where you can answer all kinds of questions relating to Kerala, Goa, Tamil Nadu and Karnataka, as well as of course the individual towns and cities of South India

TRAVEL TIPS

ARRIVAL

Most visitors to South India from the UK and the USA arrive by plane. Condor, Thomson Flights and Monarch Charter fly direct to Goa from London. Qatar Airways also operates flights from London via Doha. British Airways go to Bangalore from London in approx. 11 hrs. Serving Goa from the USA are American Airlines, Air India, Qatar Airways and US Airways. Bangalore is also served by Emirates, Lufthansa, KLM, Etihad and Air France.

BANKS & EXCHANGE

Opening times: Mon–Fri 10am–2pm, Sat 10am–noon. At many cashpoints – often even in small places – you can also withdraw rupees with your debit/credit card. If you want to change money, bureaux de change usually offer better rates than the banks. As a rule even the bank counters at the airports offer a better rate than hotels, which will always charge a hefty commission. Tip: on arrival at the airport just change a small amount of money at first and then look for a bureau de change once you've arrived at your destination. Many large shops and almost all hotels accept the usual credit cards.

CAR HIRE WITH DRIVER

It is of course much more comfortable and also safer to be chauffeured around or from hotel to hotel, rather than taking public transport. Hiring a car without a driver is definitely not recommended due the chaotic traffic and all the unwritten rules, not to mention the fact that the difference in price is very small. Always make sure that the driver speaks good English. Then he'll be able to explain a few things along the way, making the journey more interesting. Almost all travel agencies in South India arrange *chauffeured cars.* Tours can also be booked from home, complete with accommodation. Try *India Invites* in Goa *(tel. 0091 832 2715781 | www.indiain vites.com)*, or *Aries Travel* in Kerala *(tel. 0091 471 2330964 | www.ariestravel. net).*

CLIMATE, WHEN TO GO

In general, apart from the highlands, a hot, tropical climate prevails in South India. The period from November to March is the coolest and therefore the best time to travel for westerners used to cooler climes. It is pleasantly warm mornings and evenings, and the days

RESPONSIBLE TRAVEL

It doesn't take a lot to be environmentally friendly whilst travelling. Don't just think about your carbon footprint whilst flying to and from your holiday destination but also about how you can protect nature and culture abroad. As a tourist it is especially important to respect nature, look out for local products, cycle instead of driving, save water and much more. If you would like to find out more about eco-tourism please visit: *www.ecotourism.org*

From arrival to weather

Holiday from start to finish:
useful addresses and information for your trip to India

are dry and sunny. The monsoon rains come to southwest India between April and July, to the southeast between October and November.

CONSULATES & EMBASSIES

UK CONSULATE
Bangalore | Prestige Takt, 23 Kasturba Road Cross | Bangalore 560001, South India | tel. +91 80 2210 0200 | http:// ukinindia.fco.gov.uk

UK CONSULATE
Chennai | 20 Anderson Road | Chennai 600 006 | tel. +91 44 421 921 51 | Email: Consular.Chennai@fco.gov.uk

UK CONSULATE
Goa | 303–304 Casa del Sol, opposite Marriott Hotel | Miramar, Panaji 403 001 | tel. +91 832 246 1110 | Email: assistance@goaukconsular.org

US CONSULATE
Chennai | Gemini Circle | Chennai 600 006 | tel. +91 44 2857 4000 | http://chennai.usconsulate.gov/emergency.html

CURRENCY

The local currency is the Indian rupee (official abbreviation INR, unofficially Rs. One rupee is equal to 100 paise. There are coins in denominations of 10, 25 and 50 paise as well as 1, 2 and 5 rupees. Notes are in denominations of 1, 2, 5, 10, 20, 50, 100, 500 and 1000 rupees.

CUSTOMS

Currency exceeding the value of 5000 US$ must be declared on arrival. And any expensive items (e.g. video cameras) should also be declared. The import and export of Indian currency is prohibited. The following quantities may be imported in the EU (per person aged 18 or above): 200 cigarettes, 50 cigars or 250g tobacco, 1l alcohol above and 2l alcohol up to 22 vol.%, 500g coffee, other goods such as tea,

CURRENCY CONVERTER

£	INR	INR	£
1	82	10	0.12
3	246	30	0.36
5	410	50	0.46
13	1,070	130	1.58
40	3,280	400	4.87
75	6,150	750	9.13
120	9,850	1,200	14.60
250	20,500	5,000	60
500	41,000	15,000	182

$	INR	INR	$
1	55	10	0.18
3	163	30	0.55
5	271	50	0.90
13	705	130	2.40
40	2,170	400	7.35
75	4,070	750	13.80
120	6,510	1,200	22
250	13,500	5,000	92
500	27,200	15,000	275

For current exchange rates see www.xe.com

perfume and gifts up to a value of £390/574 US$.

DENTAL TREATMENT

Want to see a dentist in India? It's not such an absurd idea. The surgeries are modern, most dentists have trained in England or the USA and can carry out professional root canal treatment, perform implants, crowns and whitening. The advantage: costs are between one third and half of those in the west, there are no waiting lists, and some resorts, such as *Poovar Island Resort (tel. 0471 2573649 | www.poovarislandresort. com)* in Kerala, work together with dental surgeries. That means that after the pain comes the relaxation – a kind of reward in the form of Ayurveda or wellness treatments. Most dentists for tourists are located in Goa, followed by Kerala. Incidentally, cosmetic surgery is also a lot cheaper than in western countries.

BUDGETING

Rickshaw	£ 0.15/0.20 US$ per km; minimum of £1.25/1.50US$
Tea	£ 0.10/0.15 US$ per cup
Sun lounger	from £ 1.25/1.50 US$ with parasol rent
Dosa	from £ 0.30/0.45 US$ for one portion, stuffed
Massage	from £ 7.50/11 US$ Ayurvedic
Cinema	from £ 1/1.25 US$ for one ticket

ELECTRICITY

The usual residential power supply is 220 volt AC with a frequency of 50 Hz. There are different types of plug socket in India, so bring along a variety of adaptors. But they're also available on the spot.

GOING OUT

Many nightclubs will only admit couples. If you're single it's best to find out beforehand. Dance bars in luxury hotels are often only open to guests. Each state has different closing times and closing days for discos, nightclubs and bars, which often change. *Pub City* in Bangalore has the coolest and most stylish discos and nightclubs. In Goa, meanwhile, romantic silent parties, complete with headphones, are held on the beaches.

HEALTH

No vaccinations are necessary for visitors arriving from the UK or USA. To be on the safe side, however, you should ask your GP about inoculations against typhoid and hepatitis. A malaria prophylaxis is recommended in any event. Make sure you obtain the requisite travel insurance including cover for repatriation. In case of accident or illness in India either have your hotel call their contracted doctor or go straight to a private clinic which will provide a better standard of hygiene and medical care than the public hospitals. Because costs have to be paid up front, you need to make sure you have enough money to hand.

IMMIGRATION

Tourist visas are issued for a period of six months, and multiple visits are possible with a *multiple entry visa,* but not until two months have elapsed. If you want to return within two months, you need a *double entry visa*. Visas are issued by the respective departments of the Indian High Commission, Embassy or consulates.

HIGH COMMISSION IN LONDON:

India House, Aldwych, London WC2B 4NA, UK, tel. +44 20 7836 8484, www.hcilondon.in

EMBASSY IN NEW YORK:

2107, Massachusetts Avenue, NW, 20008 Washington D.C., District of Columbia, USA, tel. +1 202 9397 000, www.indianembassy.org

INFORMATION

INDIAN TOURIST OFFICE
7 Cork Street | WIS 3LH London | tel. 0207 43 73 677 | www.indiatouristoffice.org

1270, Avenue of the Americas | Suite 1808, 18th floor | 10020-1700 New York | tel. 0212 586-4901 | www.indiatouristoffice. org

INLAND TRAVEL

Even the remotest places in South India are accessible by public transport. The dense transport network of rail, bus and air connections works well and is inexpensive. If you're travelling long distances, apart from taking a plane, the train is the best option, principally because they are more reliable than buses, which often can't keep to their timetables because of traffic congestion. For short distances, and if you don't mind how long it takes, it's worth taking the bus for its very affordable prices. Pensioners get big reductions for bus and train travel.

The brochure 'Trains at a Glance', available from station kiosks, is very useful. Timetables, prices and available places in sleeper carriages can be found online at *www.indianrail.gov.in* and *www. iretc.com*. There are different counters for 1st, 2nd and 3rd class tickets, and often for tourists as well as women *(Ladies Ticket Office)*. Do buy your ticket before reserving your seat. It is almost impossible to book over the phone. But even when the train looks completely booked up, the so-called VIP tickets will usually be still available for a surcharge. It's necessary to make a reservation for night trains with sleeping compartments or carriages. Getting an *Indrail Pass* is only worth it in order to avoid having to stand in the queues at the ticket counters, which can get very long. Otherwise single tickets will end up a bit cheaper.

The whole country is served by a well-developed bus network. Most of the routes are covered by state-run buses, which are often hot and full. Air-conditioned buses, often Volvos, are more expensive but much more comfortable for long journeys. The categories are *ordinary* (hard seats, no air-conditioning), *deluxe* or *luxury*. Buses should at least have a fan. You can get tickets from the counters at the bus stations and, with some private bus companies, also on board.

The domestic airline market is in a constant state of flux. The former state-run Indian Airlines has now merged with Air India. New private airlines are being created while others are being closed down. At the present time there are about 10 domestic airlines operating in India, including Jet Airways *(www.jetairways. com)*, SpiceJet *(www.spicejet.com)*, GoAir *(www.goair.in)* and Paramount Airways, the latter offering only Business Class *(www.paramountairways.com)*.

INTERNET CAFÉS & WI-FI

Everywhere in India has at least one internet café. However, the connections are sometimes painfully slow. But at least the rates are very low so the length of time you're online has little bearing on the price. Meanwhile, most hotels have Wi-Fi hotspots, and its gradually becoming possible to surf in cafés and restaurants in the cities and more popular resorts.

PERSONAL SAFETY

As long as you know the rules, India is a safe destination, even for women travelling alone. The author herself has travelled all over India for many years, often on her own. Women should avoid wearing provocative clothing, and it is also not recommended to go out walking after dark. Please study the official advice before you set off.

PHONE & MOBILE PHONE

Every last village in South India has a

WEATHER IN GOA

	Jan	Feb	March	April	May	June	July	Aug	Sept	Oct	Nov	Dec
Daytime temperatures in °C/°F	32/90	32/90	30/86	33/91	33/91	30/86	29/84	29/84	29/84	31/88	33/91	33/91
Nighttime temperatures in °C/°F	20/68	20/68	23/73	25/77	26/79	24/75	24/75	24/75	24/75	24/75	22/72	20/68
Sunshine hours/day	10	9	10	10	9	4	2	4	6	7	9	10
Precipitation days/month	0	0	0	1	6	25	29	25	17	8	3	0
Water temperature in °C/°F	27/81	27/81	28/82	29/84	29/84	28/82	27/81	27/81	27/81	28/82	28/82	27/81

telephone shop from which you can easily make calls. They are marked as PCO, STD and ISD, but you can only call abroad from the ISD (International Subscriber Dialing) ones. Code from India to the UK: *0044,* to the USA *001.* Code for India: *0091.* International calls are reasonable. If you have a mobile you should use an Indian pay-as-you-go SIM card. With that you can make calls within India and back home cheaper than going through your own provider. Important: take along a copy of your passport and two passport photos.

POST

It's best to hand in your letters and postcards at hotels or post offices, rather than using a post box. Postcards, too, should be marked 'Airmail'. Sending a postcard from India to Europe costs Rs 12, a letter Rs 20, both by airmail. Post offices are open Mon–Fri 10am–6pm, Sat 10am–noon.

TAXI

Although almost all taxis are fitted with a meter, but, if possible, negotiate a fixed price beforehand. On arrival at airports and stations, it's best to take a prepaid-taxi. That way there are no arguments about the price, or extras for luggage. A more economical alternative for short distances is the motorised-rickshaw, also known as the *three-wheeler* or *tuk-tuk*. The same applies here: despite the occasional presence of a taximeter it's better to settle on a price first.

TIME DIFFERENCE

The whole of India operates to a single time zone. In winter it is 5.5 hours ahead of GMT (Greenwich Mean Time), in summer 4.5 hours ahead.

TIPPING

It is customary to tip waiters, porters, guides and drivers. The better the hotel, the more is expected. Tips are not included in bills. Always carry enough small change with you – people always want to be tipped.

TRAVEL AGENTS

IN THE UK

Audley Travel / tel. 01993 838 300 / www. audleytravel.com (includes Classic Kerala in its India itineraries); Avion Holidays / tel. 0208 449 7660 / www.avionholidays. co.uk (passionate about South India); Cox & Kings / tel. 0845 527 9374 / www.cox andkings.co.uk (long-established expertise); Exodus / tel. 0845 805 038 / www. exodus.co.uk (adventure holiday specialists, including to South India); Kerala Connections / tel. 01892 722440 / www.ker alaconnect.co.uk (tailor-made holidays in in Kerala, Tamil Nadu, Karnataka and Goa); Partnership Travel / tel. 020 8347 4020 / www.partnershiptravel.co.uk (India and South India specialists); Shoestring / tel. 01306 744797 / www.shoestring.com (for those on a tight budget); Trans Indus / tel. 0844 879 3960 / www.transindus. co.uk; Voyage Jules Verne / tel. 0845 166 7003 / www.vjv.com

IN INDIA

Also for tours, flights and accommodation throughout South India:
India Invites / Margao, Goa / tel. 0091 832 2 71 57 81 / www.indiainvites.com; Aries Travel & Holidays / Thiruvananthapuram, Kerala / tel. 0091 471 2 33 04 17 / www. ariestravel.net

NOTES

ROAD ATLAS

The green line ▬▬ indicates the Trips & Tours (p. 114–119)
The blue line ▬▬ indicates The perfect route (p. 30–31)

All tours are also marked on the pull-out map

Photo: Fishermen pulling in the nets in Kovalam

Exploring India

The map on the back cover shows how the area has been sub-divided

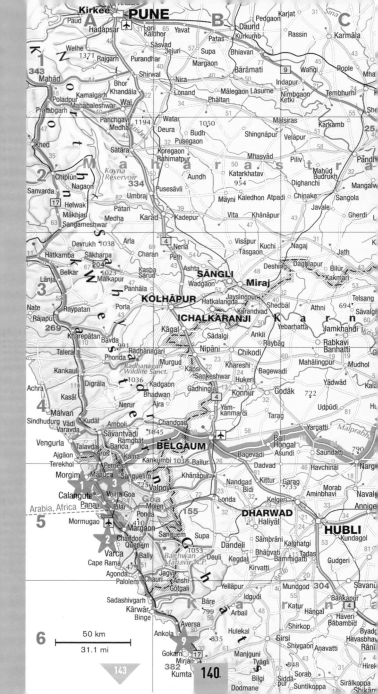

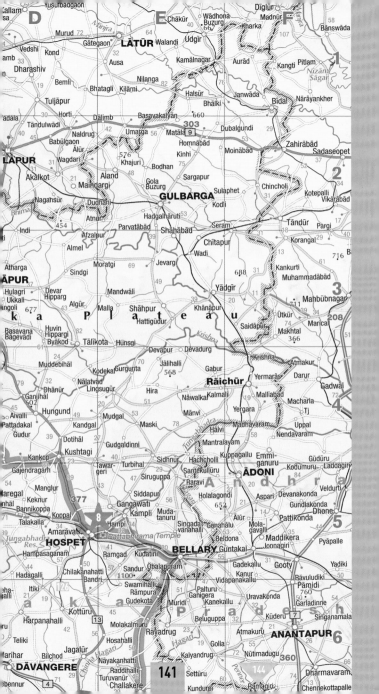

This is a map of the Deccan region of India, showing parts of Maharashtra, Karnataka, and Andhra Pradesh.

D **E** **F**

1

Yusufbādgāon
Kallam
sa
Murud 72
Gātegaon
Vedshi
Kond
amb 33
Dharashiv
19
Bemli
Tuljāpur
ādāla
Tāndulwādi
40 45
LĀPUR
31
Akālkot
Nagansūr
ĀPUR

Dīglūr
Chākūr 40
Wadhona Buzurg 66
Madnūr
Kharka
Bānswāda
64
Udgīr
107
LĀTŪR Walandi
Ausa
Kamālnagar
Aurād
Kangti Pitlam
Nizām Sāgar
Nilanga
Janwāda
Nārāyankher
Bhatagli Kilārni
Halsūr
76
Bhālki
Bidal
Dālimb
Umarga 56
Matālā 9
Dubalgundi
Naldrug 42
303
Babūlgaon
Homnābād
Moinābād
Zahīrābād
Sadaseopet
Ālūr 576
Khajuri
Kinhi
53
52 37
Wagdari
Bodhan
75
21
Aland 48
Gola Buzurg
Sargapur
Chincholi
Kotepalli
Vikarābād
Maihdargi
GULBARGA
Sulaphet
31
Dudhani
Kodli
Atnūr
Hadgalhāruti 53
Seram
Tāndūr
Pargi
Indi
454
Afzalpur
Parvatābād
Shāhābād
18
Korangal 29
40
Almel
Chitapur
13
Moratgi
Jevargi
Wadi
Kankurti
61
716
B
Sindgi
69
688
Muhammadābād
31
Atharga
Hulagri
Devar Hipparg
Mandwāli
Yādgīr
711
Mahbūbnagar
Ukkali
angoli 677
Algūr
49
Khānāpur
11
Ūtkūr 34
208
Malla
Shāhpur
39
Basavana Bagevadi
Huvin Hippargi
82
Hattigūdur
Saidāpur
Makhtal 366
Marical
Byākod
Tālīkota
Hūnsgi
Devapur
Devādurg
Krishna
51
Muddebihāl
Kodekal
Gurgunta
70
Jālihalli
568
Gabur
Krishna
Atmakūr
Darur
79
Dhānūr
Nālatvad
Lingsugūr
Hira
Rāichūr
Yermarās
Gadwāl
Ganjihāl 602
20
Nāwalka
Kalmali
Malliabad
Macharla
72
Aivalli
Hungund
49
Mudgal 53
Maski
Mānvi
Yergara
Tj
Uppal
Pattadakal
Kandgal
78
Hālvi
Mādhavaram
Nendavaram
Gudur
39
Dotihāl
Gudgaldinni
Mantralayam
58
Kankop
Kushtagi
Turbihal
Sidhnūr
Hachcholli
Kuppagallu
Emmi-ganuru
Gūdūru
Gajendragarh
23
Tawar-geri
Siruguppā
Santekullūru
Raravi
ĀDONI
Kodumuru
Laddagiri
54
Manglur
Siddapur
56
Holalagondi
Aspari
Devanakonda
Velderti
aregal
Keknur
377
Bannikoppa
Koppal
Gangāwāti
Kampli
Mudatanuru
652
21
Ālūr
Gundlakonda
Dhone
14
Pattikonda
Talakala
Hampi
34
Singada-vanahalli
Gonahalli
Mola-gavalli
44
Pyāpalle
Amarāvati
Beldona
Maddikera
Jonnagiri
Tungabhadra Res.
Pattabhirama Temple
HOSPET
Guntakal
Hampasaganam
Rāmgad
Kudatini
BELLARY
Gadekallu
Gooty
Yadiki
Hadagalli
57
Sandur 1100°
Obalapuram
Kanur
Rāvuludiki
Chilakanahatti
Bandri
Vidapanakallu
Pāmidi 760
50
Itiki
Swamihalli
Rāmpura
Palturu
Ganigera
Kanekallu
Uravakonda
Garladinne
Singanamala
Kottūru
45
Gudekota
Muridi
Beluguppa
Kūderu 7
126
13
Molakalmuru
Harpanahalli
Hosahalli
Rāyadrug
23
Atmakurū
ANANTAPUR
6
Teliki
Jagalūr
Hagari
19
Golla
55
26
360
Bilchod
Nāyakanhatti
141
Kalyandrug
Nūtimadugu
DĀVANGERE
Raddihalli
Turuvanūr
Challakere
144
Dharmavaram
4 71
Settūru
Penneru
Chennekottapalle
bennur
Kundurū
Rāmagiri

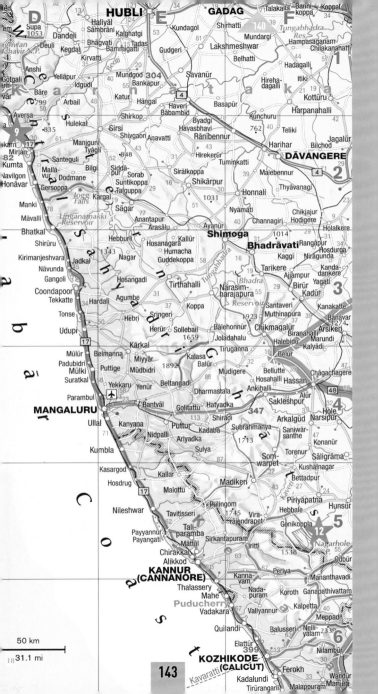

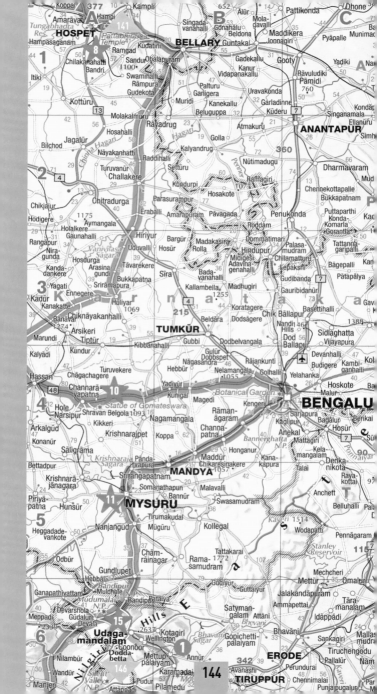

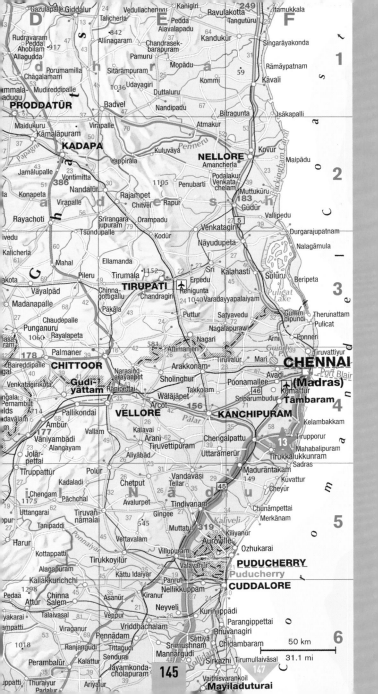

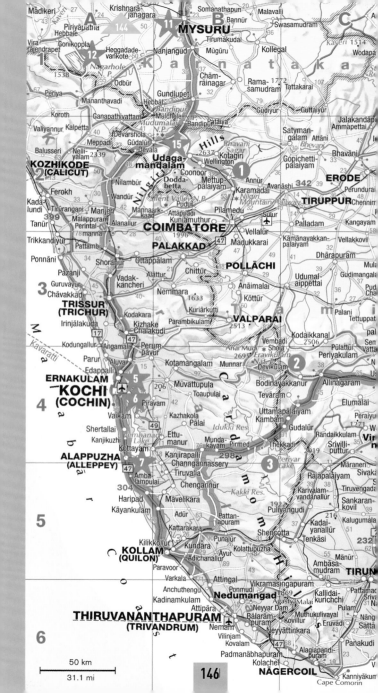

A
Mādikeri 27 24
Krishnarā-
jānagara 50
144 11
MYSURU
Somanāthapun 20
Bannūr
Malavalli
Swasamudram

Piriyāpatna
Hebbāle
12 Heggadade-
vankote
Nanjangūd
Tirumakudal
Mūgūru
Kollegal
Kaveri 1514 C
Wodapa

Vira-
rajendrapet
Gonikoppal
Nagarhole
N. P.
1538
Odbūr
Chām-
rāinagar
Rama-
samudram
1772
Tattakarai
107

Periya
67
Mānanthavadi
Ganapathivattam
Gundlupet
32

Koroth
Hebbal
Bandipur
N.P.
Gūdiyur
Guttaiyūr

Valiyannur Kalpetta
40
Meppadi
Dēvarshola
Gūdalūr
Mudumalai
N.P.
Bandipi
Pataiya
Satyman-
galam Attani
Jalakandap
Ammapettai

Balusseri Nelli-
yalam 2339
KOZHIKODE
(CALICUT) 2
Udaga-
mandalam
Hills
Kotagiri
Wellington 2637
Coonoor
Bhavāni
nagar
Bhevani
Gōpichetti-
palaiyam
33
Bhavāni

Ferokh
30
Nilambur
Dodda-
betta
Mettupalaiyam
Annūr
Avanāshi 342
39
ERODE
Perundurai
48

Kada-
lundi Tirūrangani
Wandūr
Manjeri 42
Silent Valley N.P.
Karamadai
TIRUPPUR
Chennin

Tanūr 399
Malappuram
Perintal
manna
Alanallur
Mannaarkkaad
Pudut
Pilamedu
Nilgiri
Mountain Railway
53
Sulur
Palladam
29
Kangayam

Trikkandiyūr
Pattambi 78
Kuniamuthur
COIMBATORE
1996
Vellalūr
Kāmānayakkan-
palaiyam
Vellakkovil

Ponnāni
34
Shoranūr
Ottappālam
Madukkarai 47
32
Dhārapuram

Pazanji
Vadak-
kancheri
Alāttur
Chittūr
POLLĀCHI
41
Mula

Guruvayur
45
Nemmara
29
Anāimalai
Udumal-
aippettai
Gudimangala
37

Chāvakkad 40
1633
Kōttūr
36
Pud
Cha

TRISSUR
(TRICHUR) 3
Kodakara
Kuriākutti
VALPARAI
2513
Palani
Tettuppat
pal

Irinjālakuda
Kizhake
Chalakudi
Parambikulam
Kodaikkanal
2506
Sem
Vatta

Kavaratti 17
Kodungallur Angamāli
47
Perum-
pavur
Anai Mudi
2695
Eravikulam
Nat P. Shola
Pulāttūr
Periyakulam
N

Parur Aluva
Kotamangalam
Munnar
Devikulam
2
38
U

ERNAKULAM
KOCHI
(COCHIN) 4
Edappalli 5
6
206
Mūvattupula
Toaupulai
Bodinayakkanur
Tevāram
Allināgaram

Vaikam
Kazhakola
Pālai
Uttamapālaiyam
Kambam
Elumalai
Peraiyu

Shertallai
Kanjikuzhi
Kottayam 49
Ettu-
manur
Munda-
kayam Pirmed
Idukki Res.
Gudalūr
Randaikkulam
Srivilli-
puttur 35
1271
Vir
n

ALAPPUZHA
(ALLEPPEY) 7
Kanjirapalli
Channgannassery
Tiruvalla 298
Thēkkadi
2919
Māraneri
Sivaka

Ambalampulai 304
Chengannur
Kakki Res.
Periyar
Lake 3
Rājapālaiyam
39
Karivalam-
vandanallur
Tiruvengada
Sankaran-
kovil

Haripad
Māvelikara
1922
Puliyangudi
216
Kalugumala
51

Kāyankulam
Adūr 63
Pattan-
apuram
Kadai-
yanallūr 232

5
Kattakara
Punalūr
Shencotta
Tenkāsi
55
Mānūr
62

Kilikkōllūr
Kundara
Kolattupuzha
Ambāsa-
mudram
TIRUN

KOLLAM
(QUILON)
Adichanallur 89
Ayur
Paravoor
Varkala
Attingal
Vikramasingapuram

Anchuthengu
Kadinamkulam
Attipāra
Ponmudi
Nedumangad
1869
Agasty Malai
Kallidai-
kurichchi
Pattam
Sriva
31 N

THIRUVANANTHAPURAM
(TRIVANDRUM) 6
Bālarām-
puram
Neyyar Dam
Nemam Muthukulivayal
Eruvadi Pulam
Nāng
Satta

Vilinjam
Kovalam
Neyyāttinkara

Padmanābhapuram
Kolachel
47 58
Alagiāpandi-
puram 23
Panakudi

50 km
31.1 mi
146
NĀGERCOIL
Kanniyakuru
Cape Comorin

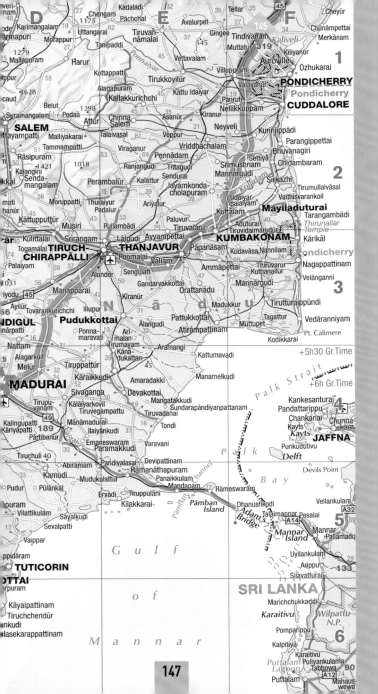

KEY TO ROAD ATLAS

Autobahn, mehrspurige Straße - in Bau / Highway, multilane divided road - under construction	═══ ═ ═ ═	Autoroute, route à plusieurs voies - en construction / Autosnelweg, weg met meer rijstroken - in aanleg
Fernverkehrsstraße - in Bau / Trunk road - under construction	▬▬▬ ▬ ▬ ▬	Route à grande circulation - en construction / Weg voor interlokaal verkeer - in aanleg
Hauptstraße / Principal highway	———	Route principale / Hoofdweg
Nebenstraße / Secondary road	———	Route secondaire / Overige verharde wegen
Fahrweg, Piste / Practicable road, track	———	Chemin carrossable, piste / Weg, piste
Straßennummerierung / Road numbering	E20 11 70 26 5 40 9	Numérotage des routes / Wegnummering
Entfernungen in Kilometer / Distances in kilometers	259 130 129	Distances en kilomètres / Afstand in kilometers
Höhe in Meter - Pass / Height in meters - Pass	1365 • ‿	Altitude en mètres - Col / Hoogte in meters - Pas
Eisenbahn - Eisenbahnfähre / Railway - Railway ferry	▬▬▬ ········	Chemin de fer - Ferry-boat / Spoorweg - Spoorpont
Autofähre - Schifffahrtslinie / Car ferry - Shipping route	———	Bac autos - Ligne maritime / Autoveer - Scheepvaartlijn
Wichtiger internationaler Flughafen - Flughafen / Major international airport - Airport	✈ ✈	Aéroport importante international - Aéroport / Belangrijke internationale luchthaven - Luchthaven
Internationale Grenze - Provinzgrenze / International boundary - Province boundary	▬▬▬▬▬	Frontière internationale - Limite de Province / Internationale grens - Provinciale grens
Unbestimmte Grenze / Undefined boundary	▬▬ ▬▬ ▬▬	Frontière d'Etat non définie / Rijksgrens onbepaalt
Zeitzonengrenze / Time zone boundary	-4h Greenwich Time ·········· -3h Greenwich Time	Limite de fuseau horaire / Tijdzone-grens
Hauptstadt eines souveränen Staates / National capital	**MANILA**	Capitale nationale / Hoofdstad van een souvereine staat
Hauptstadt eines Bundesstaates / Federal capital	**Kuching**	Capitale d'un état fédéral / Hoofdstad van een deelstat
Sperrgebiet / Restricted area	▭	Zone interdite / Verboden gebied
Nationalpark / National park	▭	Parc national / Nationaal park
Antikes Baudenkmal / Ancient monument	∴	Monument antiques / Antiek monument
Sehenswertes Kulturdenkmal / Interesting cultural monument	* Angkor Wat	Monument culturel interéssant / Bezienswaardig cultuurmonument
Sehenswertes Naturdenkmal / Interesting natural monument	* Ha Long Bay	Monument naturel interéssant / Bezienswaardig natuurmonument
Brunnen / Well	‿	Puits / Bron
Ausflüge & Touren / Trips & Tours	▬▬▬	Excursions & tours / Uitstapjes & tours
Perfekte Route / Perfect route	▬▬▬	Itinéraire idéal / Perfecte route
MARCO POLO Highlight	★ 1	MARCO POLO Highlight

INDEX

The index includes all the places, excursion destinations and beaches, as well as important terms and persons described in the guide. Page numbers in bold indicate the main entry.

WRITE TO US

e-mail: info@marcopologuides.co.uk

Did you have a great holiday?
Is there something on your mind?
Whatever it is, let us know!
Whether you want to praise, alert us to errors or give us a personal tip – MARCO POLO would be pleased to hear from you.
We do everything we can to provide the very latest information for your trip.

Nevertheless, despite all of our authors' thorough research, errors can creep in. MARCO POLO does not accept any liability for this. Please contact us by e-mail or post.

MARCO POLO Travel Publishing Ltd
Pinewood, Chineham Business Park
Crockford Lane, Chineham
Basingstoke, Hampshire RG24 8AL
United Kingdom

PICTURE CREDITS
Cover Photograph: Kerala, houseboat, Getty Images: Photononstop (Cheuva)
Images: Gallery Sumukha: Premilla Baid (16 bottom); D. Gehm (1 bottom, 15, 20, 112); Huber: Limmatdruck (26 l.), Ripani (10/11, 67, 128 bottom, 142, 149), Schmid (flap l., 2 centre bottom, 32/33, 34, 37, 38, 43); Ishu Datwani: Farrokh Chothia (17 bottom); Junkyard Groove (16 top); O. Krüger (flap r., 3 top, 3 centre, 3 bottom, 8, 9, 22, 29, 40, 44, 44/45, 45, 51, 52, 55, 57, 60, 62, 69, 72, 73, 74/75, 76, 86, 89, 90, 93, 94/95, 100/101, 103, 105, 107, 109, 110, 114/115, 116, 117, 124, 126, 126/127, 127, 128 top, 129); Laif: hemis.fr (96), Huber (28/29, 59, 72/73, 82, 85), Jonkmanns (120/121), Lewis (2 centre top, 7, 81); K. Maeritz (12/13, 18/19, 28, 78, 99, 124/125, 125, 138/139); mauritius images: Alamy (2 top, 2 bottom, 4, 5, 6, 24/25, 26 r., 30 l., 30 r., 46/47), CuboImages (118), ib (Krüger) (27, 71), ib (Tack) (65); Sujay Shastry (16 centre); S. Verma (123); Dr Vishwanath: S. Laxminarayan (17 top)

1st Edition 2013
Worldwide Distribution: Marco Polo Travel Publishing Ltd, Pinewood, Chineham Business Park, Crockford Lane, Basingstoke, Hampshire RG24 8AL, United Kingdom. Email: sales@marcopolouk.com
© MAIRDUMONT GmbH & Co. KG, Ostfildern
Chief editors: Michaela Lienemann (concept, managing editor), Marion Zorn (concept, text editor)
Author: Dagmar Gehm; Editor: Christina Sothmann
Programme supervision: Anita Dahlinger, Ann-Katrin Kutzner, Nikolai Michaelis
Picture editor: Gabriele Forst
What's hot: wunder media, Munich;
Cartography road atlas: © MAIRDUMONT, Ostfildern; Cartography pull-out map: © MAIRDUMONT, Ostfildern
Design: milchhof : atelier, Berlin; Front cover, pull-out map cover, page 1: factor product munich
Translated from German by Tony Halliday, Oxford; editor of the English edition: Paul Fletcher, Suffolk
Prepress: BW-Medien GmbH, Leonberg

DOS & DON'TS

A few things to bear in mind when travelling in South India

DON'T UNDERESTIMATE THE UNDERTOW

Regardless of whether you do water-sports or simply want to go swimming in the sea, it is vital to check out beforehand whether and where there is any dangerous undertow. When swimming, it's best to stick to the sections of beach designated as bathing areas and avoid unfamiliar waters.

DON'T BEHAVE AGGRESSIVELY

In India people react with complete bewilderment when foreigners raise their voices out of impatience or anger and lose their temper with others. Such behaviour is considered a sign of lack of self-control and as being uncouth. Go ahead and say clearly what the problem is, but without getting too agitated.

DON'T SHOW YOUR FEET

As many westerners can't sit cross-legged very well, after a while they tend to stretch out one or the other leg and almost inevitably end up pointing the sole of their foot towards somebody else. However, that is considered extremely impolite in India.

DON'T DRESS INAPPROPRIATELY

Nude sunbathing is officially forbidden, but many women tourists still take their tops off at the beach or pool. They shouldn't be surprised about any curious onlookers. Women who try to visit a temple with strap tops or short shorts

will either be refused admission or lent some material with which to cover their shoulders and/or legs. Also adult women wearing mini-skirts evoke considerable disapproval. The same goes for men who enter hotels and restaurants without a shirt on. A good tip for women: with the *salwar kameez* – the long, loose-fitting tunic over tapering trousers – you'll always be dressed appropriately.

DON'T USE YOUR LEFT HAND

It is considered unclean. So only use the fingers of your right hand when you want to eat like the Indians do, namely without cutlery. The left hand stays firmly on your lap. Nor should gifts be presented with the left hand.

DON'T ENTER HOLY PLACES WEARING SHOES

It isn't just temples, pagodas and mosques that you shouldn't enter with shoes on, but museums and private houses as well. Getting your shoes looked after on dedicated shelves or counters only costs a few rupees. If you don't want to go barefoot, you can still wear socks.

DON'T DISPLAY AFFECTION IN PUBLIC

Indians are on the prudish side. Young couples now hold hands in public, but kissing and smooching outdoors are completely taboo. It violates the code of modesty, and holidaymakers should respect that.